YAKUP ALMELEK

Don't Make Me Laugh

NEWIDEABOOKS

First paperback edition October 2020

Publications Coordinator
Atakan Kelleci

Book Cover Designer
Gonca Küçük

Graphics Designer
Meral Gök

Don't Make Me Laugh / Yakup Almelek
ISBN (paperback) 978-1-8381587-0-5

Published by NEW IDEA BOOKS LTD
www.newideabooks.co.uk
info@newideabooks.co.uk
59 Edgecot Grove, Seven Sisters
LONDON   N15 5HE

YAKUP ALMELEK

Don't Make Me Laugh

YAKUP ALMELEK

Yakup Almelek was born in 1936 in Ankara. Besides his business life, he carried out his cultural, artistic and literistic activities with a great passion.

The author published his columns in a number of newspapers including Cumhuriyet and Şalom for many years. His short story called "My weekly Wage is Five Liras" was adapted as a short film and shown in the 42nd Antalya Golden orange Film Festival. His plays called "The Businessman", "The Awakening" and "Vendetta" were staged şn New York Broadway.

The author's plays, columns, stories and poetry were translated into English and published both in Turkish and English.

Yakup Almelek was awarded with the "İsmet Küntay Theater Special Awars" at the 40th İsmet Küntay Theater Awards with his play "Awakening" stayed by the Oyun Bandı during the 2014 – 2015 season. In 2016, with his bold, pioneering and fresh vision he used all his means and his estate to found the Kültüral Performing Arts.

Yakup Almelek, who is a PEN Club Turkey member keeps on being productive in the fields of culture, art and theater.

Contents

HAROLD PINTER

The "2005 Nobel Prize of Literature" was awarded to the British playwright Harold Pinter. Harold Pinter -may God grant him a long life- is 75 years old. (1 Harold Pinter died on December 24, 2008. Among his books translated into our language are Betrayal, Party Time, Moonlight, Celebration and The Dumb Waiter)

In this beautiful art called literature, 75 seems to be the ideal age to receive a little fortune over 1 million Dollars from the Swedish, isn't it? May he enjoy it. It was probably not easy for him to arrive to these days. Heaven knows which artistic calamities he survived, how he exerted himself mentally and how many times he was beaten down on by critics.

Who is Harold Pinter? First we should get to know him. Let Harold Pinter tell about Harold Pinter, with his own words, with his own style. This way, let's give to Caesar what is Caesar's. Unbeknown, mysterious, talking barely and laconically, on the other hand, short-tempered, grumpy and peevy, rough and acrimonious, with a particular taste for thorny words. Thus Pinter would have drawn his own portrait with the talent of a master painter. "I am all of those I have cited," he would say, "but with an artistic side. Please see that side. Do not make much of my flaws. Enjoy what I give and forget about what I couldn't. Be it a poem, a play or a scenario of mine; the aftertaste must be good. They should let you confront realities. I should excite you with what I say."

These are the truths of Pinter. He accepts his flaws with a great sincerity. But he warns his audience: "You should consider my talents too."He is writing since 45 years. With desire and excitement, picturing the bitterest truths with the simplest word of daily life. See where his journey arrived. He has one such memory: He started to write in 1957. His first play "The Birthday Party" was chastised by the critics. And he felt sorry. So he went to the theater, eight days after the work was staged for the first time. There were only six people in the theater. And apparently they were not happy about what they had seen. The gate of that day was two Pounds and eight Shillings. What a great tragedy it is for a playwrigt, is that not? Not being watched!

The roots of the name Pinter reach back to "Pinta". According to the conjectures of a relative, the origins of the family stem from the Jews who migrated from Spain and Portugal. Pinta was supposedly a well-known family in Lissabon. However, there is no evidence backing up this argument. According to the aunts of Pinter, they must have immigrated to London from Russia or Poland.

One of the best-known plays of Pinter is "Betrayal". I watched this play in London. There were three players, a lady and two gentlemen. The fourth person existed only through talks, but he was not present at the stage. Two interesting points stroke my eye. First, the play interprets the sex-based companionship between two married couples living in London between 1968 and 1977. The story plays back from the end date 1977 untill the start date 1968, step by step. First the outcome is presented. Then the audience is shown how things arrived at this outcome. A different turn of expression!

Secret relationships between two married couples are not considered ethical, but who can deny realities? Let's not bury our heads into the sand like an ostrich does. Since theater is the epitoome of life (!). The second point is Harold Pinter's way of addressing to the most complex issues with a simple style. Pinter does not seek refuge in long, pompous sentences. Whatever he wants to say, he says it with words from the daily life. And thanks to it the twenty nine plays he has written so far still keep their actualness.

Ultimately, Pinter is a foolproof and interesting writer.

Source: Harold Pinter's speech when he received the David Cohen Prize for Literature and his play "Betrayal".

42TH GOLDEN ORANGE FILM FESTIVAL

The film business is not quite my field of interest. It is also quite far from my hobbies. But since seven days my wife and I are watching the 42th Golden Orange Film Festival with pleasure. My dear friend from the newspaper, Victor Apalaçi informs us every week about the must-see movies. Despite his sorrow that we all share, we know he will evaluate the festival movies professionally.

My objective is however a little different...

I would like to dedicate this article of mine to the festival gossip. Gossip is the sweetest food of the world! No chocolate can compete with the taste of gossip, making you talk about topics such as "he said this and she said that, who was caught with whom and where and how". Now let's leave the philosophical depth of gossip aside and focus on visual examples:

The granddaughter of the genius Charile Chaplin was in Antalya. According to the authorities, Kiera is the seventh most beautiful woman on the planet. Why not first but seventh? It requires tactfulness to select beauties. Which difference(s) exist between Kiera and those who came the first until the sixth? Do we think it is easy to define beauty? It is not fit to a columnist to talk big. But if you ask me, they were unjust to the poor girl. She was chatting with someone, two meters away from me. The sveltness of her face reflected to her elegance, and her kindness to her demeanor. The theme of the painting was perfection. O Jury! I leave you alone with your conscience.

Now the hot news. Kiera disputed with her fiancé, they even quarelled.

This was always difficult for me to get. Fiancés will have ample time to quarrel once they are married. Why so much tension already?

If they do it for training purposes, then it is fine for me. Kiera resembles her grandfather. She loves to make movies. She will apparently remain in Antalya after the festival for research. You never know! Maybe she will bestow another "Limelight" to the world of hearts.

The orange trees in Antalya shook with another news. Woody Harrelson and Michael Madsen saluted each other with fists. They told those who tried to separate them that they were inseparable. The next day Michael Madsen decided that the town was too hot for him and he hit the plane. The moment the wheels left the ground, a smell of alcohol invaded the air. According to certain external sources, whose only job is to bandy, the main reason of the fight is what I will tell below.

Years ago, a role of a killer was given to Madsen. During the rehearsals the producer gave up on the idea for some reason and announced that he preferred Harrelson. So, the main role was taken away from one and given to the other. Hell broke loose. Madsen declared war to both the producer and Harrelson and ever since, he shows his deep sympathy wherever he encounters them.

"There is yet another possibility" is the first line of a song, but it also fits the issue on hand. Apparently, both Harrelson and Madsen had eyes on a very beautiful young girl. She was a fine lady, the kind the Ottoman poets wrote about, slender as a cypress tree, smooth like a rose petal, an elegant creature. Since the girl chose Harrelson as he was taller, Madsen was quite sore. Once you are sore, it is hard to feel good again.

The main objective of gossip is to backbite and to entertain this way. TV channels and newspapers offer us ample amounts of material to have a good time.

So I too wanted to offer you a bouquet. Isn't that amazing to observe gossip from various perspectives?

RESURRECTION BLUES

Arthur Miller did not like to comment about his plays. Before "Death of a Salesman" was staged for the first time, someone asked him what his play is about. Miller's answer was: "The play is about a salesman and at the end he dies." It is not hard to guess how satisfactory this answer was for the questioner.

Many plays by Miller were staged in our country by public and private theaters and they all received great interest. "Crucible", "Death of a Salesman", "The Price", "All My Sons" were all crown jewels of our theaters. Miller was not only a good writer but someone who loved to live and who knew how to live. Wouldn't his marriage to the blond superstar Marilyn Monroe among all the daily grind prove my point?

The fact that Monroe chose Arthur Miller as her husband shows that far from being depicted as a sex bomb, she was an intelligent woman who prized quality and value. If the expression fits here, let's say well done to both of them!

Unfortunately the two are no longer among us. We lost Miller last year. He was an irreplaceable talent in the theatrical enlightenment. (Editor's Note: Arthur Miller died on February 10, 2005)

Arthur Miller wrote a play when he was 86 and named it "Resurrection Blues". The dictionnaries define the word "resurrection" as "revival and coming back to life". The play started to be staged the same year, namely on August 9th 2002 at the Guthrie Theater in Minneapolis.

All Miller plays are dramas. The individual's responsibility towards the society and the demeanor the society has to show towards the individual were always the main issue in his plays. No societal unit or person has the luxury of saying "I am just an audience, I do not participate." Since Miller treated these topics with the meticulousness of a diamond-cutter, he is a highly valued playwright.

"Resurrection Blues" happens in a South American dictatorship. United States is supporting this regime. Violence and drug use have gotten in the society's blood. Two per cent of the society possessed ninety-six per cent of the wealth. The society secretly yearns for a saviour and prays for it. Finally, someone coming from the countryside claims he is the son of God and that he will save them all. However, he is arrested by the governing power. At the end of the trial he is found guilty and was punished by crucifixion. Why crucifixion and not being shot to death?

The presiding judge was of the opinion that it is necessary to find interesting alternatives in an environment where thousands were shot to death, hence he selected crucifixion.

Miller claimed that he gave emphasis to humour in this play, unlike the others: "The audience follows me with seriousness, they have convinced themselves that there is nothing to laugh about in my plays, however "Resurrection Blues" will be a novelty." Or: "If they do not laugh while watching this play, I will start thinking that there is something wrong with them."

With his play, Miller is also -let's use a humourous, slang expression- heaping ridicule upon people's fondness of money. And he also says that this "fondness has turned into madness". The deification of money constitutes the main theme of the play. Buying and selling became everything for the human mind anyway!

We commercialize everything we look at and everything we see. But we are not satisfied with it, so we privatize them. Miller condemns this insatiable ambition not only with this play, but also with his articles. In one article he mentions "Let's make the executions in stadiums and sell each seat for at least 300 dollars". In another he states "Congress members shall sell the votes they will cast to make laws in accordance with the desires of private companies."These are paraphrases from his articles published in New York Times.

The American society is seeminly not thinking about judging Arthur Miller for his accusations. Maybe because they think he is not entirely wrong. Let's hope that "Resurrection Blues" finds a place at our theaters too. I am sure an incident happening in one South American country will appeal to theTurkish audience's mind and soul. The play will be staged this season at the Old Vic Theater in London Waterloo, between February 14-April 22.

I used the original name of the play as a title. The person translating the play shall decide about the right title in Turkish.

THE GIRL WITH
THE MOUNTAIN BIKE

Hakan saw that girl in Belgrad Forest for the first time.

She was climbing uphill with a mountain bike. That hill was too steep for a simple bicycle. And Hakan was descending walking. The bike the girl used while climbing opposite to Hakan was the newest model according to what newspapers described. Their eyes just crossed. The girl smiled sweetly and said "Goodmorning" And from Hakan's mouth a sincere word of good morning dropped. The girl hit the pedals and the bike finally reached the end of the slope.

It was a saturday, the weather was neither too hot nor too cold. It was around 11 o'clock. Hakan was wearing sporty chic blue trainers. He had perspired. He was walking, then halting a bit, than running. He could only make one fourth of the six kilometers track so far. His target was to complete twelve kilometers.

He was coming to the forest a few times per year. Sometimes with his friends and sometimes alone. He liked the perfume coming from the pine trees a lot. Trees were his modest sweethearts, that he enjoyed so much to watch. That morning he was going to meet a friend. But his friend had a last minute obligation and could not accompany him to the forest. Both liked to jog in the forest. When his friend told him on the phone that he was not going to make it, Hakan decided to not change his plan. He was alone in the forest and he did not regret it. However, he was feeling languished, it was a heaviness he could not really find a reason for.

He started to jog slowly. He thought about his job for a while. Then he gave up thinking. He searched hopelessly for a topic to busy his mind while running. Suddenly the shade of the girl's bike appeared on the turf. He lifted his head, when their gaze crossed, he saluted her. They both smiled. Hakan was looking more carefully at the girl now. She was wearing blue jeans and a green t-shirt. Hakan, whose favourite color was green, told himself, "Our color choices seem to match". The girl apparently liked sports as well. Otherwise, why would she come with her mountain bike over there. What would she do on these pathways under massive trees?

He felt like talking. It would be so nice if he could chat a bit and find a company for this short waldeinsamkeit. They would chit chat. He would tell about his job, she would maybe talk about her life. She might be a university student. Maybe she was working. Being a family girl would fit her well too. "Whatever she is, she carries it gracefully," he thought.

He looked behind him. The girl was far away now, looking like a little spot.

It is actually not very easy to establish contact with Turkish girls. If you want to get close to them by chatting, they suddenly invent sex-oriented worries about you. They think: "Does this guy want to take me to the bed?" they wonder. And they want to inject this thought to guys, sometimes with their words and sometimes with their movements. It is best to keep away from our girls and to give them the initiative. Let them decide on their own and approach the males. Wither sexual, or verbal... Whatever their beautiful and sweet souls feel like...

Hakan's and his imaginary friend's thoughts were moving in this direction. On the other hand, European ladies were so relaxed... No doubt they also had some unbreakable taboos and unattainable obstacles about sex. What differed them from our girls was that they could talk about everything readily and easily. Our girls' taboos, caused by social pressures, were much more solid. Hakan was walking and philosophizing about the other sex and bedroom taboos. Moreover, he was producing thoughts about the girl with the mountain bike.

"Do I have the right to do this?" he asked himself. He felt he was immersed into unjust thoughts. How could he become taken by such weird thoughts without knowing someone, without even exchanging couple of words with her? He mumbled with his heart, "I want to talk to this girl, to be friends with her, shortly, to get to know her!"

"If she doesn't feel like, she doesn't hold my hand, I'd sit by her side and we could talk for a while," he thought.

Hakan had surrendered to his fate anyway. If only the girl with the mountain bike was of the same opinion. He was tired. He searched for a bench on the way. Maybe the girl would see Hakan and stop by. She would lean her fancy bike on a tree and come by his side. "Hello!" she would say. And Hakan would answer readily: "Hello!"

"Are you tired?" she would probably ask. And he would reply, "Yes I am tired indeed, would you like to sit for a moment?" And then maybe the girl would sit by his side and the sweet conversational feast would start. Suddenly he had the idea that she was possibly not turkish. He chased the worry quickly off his mind, "So what, then we can speak English." Unfortunately, there was not a single bench on the road he was walking. The municipality was literally preventing him from meeting the girl. Suddenly he turned his head towards the pathway and saw the bike. The girl was completing her fourth round and he was just somewhere in the middle of his first. When she was passing by him, the girl shook her head. "Take it easy," she said. Then she roamed away, pedalling with ease and harmony. Hakan was all sunshine now. The girl had spoken to him!

Hakan felt delighted and promised himself. He was going to talk back to her on the fifth round and invite her to sip a tea at the little coffeehouse at the entrance. "Nothing can stop me, I want to get to know this girl. I should definitely talk to her," he thought. As she was riding her bike, he could not really see whether she was tall or small, plump or thin. These were all trivial details now. Lost in the fog of his thoughts, he started to jog slowly. As he was advancing on the parcours, he saw the girl walking, trailing her bike by her side. The girl was looking in front of her and walked straight towards Hakan. Then he saw her well and observed her at a glance. She was rather plump, around 1m60.

Hakan was shivering now. He did not expect to encounter her all of a sudden. A "Hello" fell off his lips. And the girl answered "Hello". Then she jumped on her bike and pedalled away at a lighning speed.

Hakan was flabbergasted. He had not been able to tell anything except saying hello. Nbow he was bitter at himself, he was sorry for not being able to start a conversation. What could be the worse? She could say, "I don't have time, my husband, fiancé or boyfriend is waiting for me now. Have a nice day". She looked like a sincere person, she would never make him feel bad about himself. Indeed, you never knew about women. They were mostly like a wavy sea. Moreover, if she is really engaged or married? He could not even see whether she was wearing a ring.

Hakan was naive and he expected his counterpart to act in the same way. Now he was decided. No matter what her marital status was, you could always invite someone over a tea. This last idea lightened his soul. With the winds of this cool idea, he quickened his pace. On the other hand, he was rehearsing every sentence he was going to tell to the girl. If the girl was spoiled and wicked? Maybe. But there was no way back now. He was envisageing all possibilities. Half an hour passed. She did not reappear. He walked yet another half hour. His eyes were searching for the shade of a far away bicycle. He was all ears just to hear the pedals. But the girl had vanished!

"Maybe something happened to her!" he thought aloud. This was a weak chance. There would be a lot of people running or jogging in the Belgrad Forests on a weekend. Seen from this perspective, a young girl could happily do her sports. But where was she? He decided to return and stop by the little cafe. Maybe she was tired, or maybe she just stopped to relax and visit the loo. He went in. There was no one else than the old waiter.

He sat down on a chair and drank a bottle of ice cold water. If he chatted with the waiter, maybe he would learn a thing or two about the girl with the mountain bike. It was the waiter who started the conversation. "Buddy, it would do good against sweat and fatigue, would you like to have a fresh, strong tea?"

The innkeeper's friendly attempt was kind. Hakan answered in the same sincerity. "Thanks, uncle, of course, I'd like to."

The man was a real tea professional, no doubt about it. His ways of washing the tea glass in hot water, of pouring the red tea into the glass proved it all. And he was a talkie too. His communication skills must have been most welcome by his guests.

"Something annoying just happened, son" the tea man started to tell. The moment these words fell from his mouth, Hakan dropped the tea glass off his hand and spilled tea onto the table. The old, experienced tea man was surprised and asked Hakan, "So you know the girl too?" Hakan answered, "No, I don't. I just saw her while strolling around." While cleaning the table and refreshing the tea, the old men went on to tell.

"Such a sweet girl. I could say, much better behaved than my own grandchild. As a giant pine cone rolls in front of her, she brakes and the bike slides off. She rolls on the ground, her trousers get torn and her knees are scratched badly. And seeing her knees bleed, she starts crying. Fortunately she thought about coming to me."

Hakan asked, unable to suppress his excitement and anxiety. "What did you do? Which knee was it and how is she now?" "What did I do, let me tell. I was a medic while doing my military service. So, I know a bit about these issues. I told her, "Beautiful granddughter, you do not need to worry. Now pull your jeans up until your knee."So I cleaned the would, neutralized it and applied wound cream before dressing it. She was hurting, but she is so smart and courageous. I said, "Come on, granddaughter. Let's load your bike to your car. You'd better return home and show that wound to a doctor just in case. Maybe it is infected. I did my best, but you never know."

Hakan asked, "And then?" The tea man went on to tell cheerfully. "You see son, I have all my first aid material in that cupboard. Whenever something bad happens, may Allah forbid, I can help. At least the wounded can then go to the hospital comfortably." Hakan repeated his question, "And then, what happened?"

The tea man told... "She drove away. He wanted to pay me money. I said 'No way granddaughter. Come again with your husband or your fiancé, and bring me some Turkish delights if you want." And he added "Her health is more important than anything else." Hakan was all ears now. "And how did she reply?"

"She is apparently a very decent girl. She said 'I am not married, nor do I have a fiancé. But I would like to pay you for your help." I said: "Granddaughter, bring me your wedding invitation when you are going to get married, then we are even. She gave me fifty liras anyway. She said, she is going to invite me if she marries one day, and drove away."

Hakan was enthusiastic now. So the girl was single. At least, officially. Suddenly his good mood turned into anger. "So what, what's that got to do with me?" he told himself.

He asked the tea man: "So, uncle, what was this girl's name?"

The answer came swiftly. "I don't know, son, never asked..."

Hakan, "I wonder where she is living."

"If only I knew. I never thought about asking."

What should Hakan do now? Nothing, apparently. He did not know anything about the girl, except that she was neither married nor engaged. He was at a loss. It was just a girl he saw five times riding her bike, and once he had said hello to her. Now he was feeling nervous, curious and heavy with an uneasy anxiety sinking down his heart.

The silence was short-lived and Hakan kept on asking. "So, was it the first time she came over here?"

The tea-man said, "No, no. It's not the first time, I had seen her a few times before. In fact, she would never talk, she would just drink a tea and bid goodbye. Oh, another thing. She always appears on Sundays. It was the first time I saw her on Saturday."

Hakan took a look at his watch. It was too early to return now. He had lost his lust for walk. The girl was defiling in front of his eyes now. Her image was not going anywhere. He wanted to return. Then he realized that the tea man was observing him carefully.

While paying for the tea, he asked, "Uncle, I have a request from you. I'm going to note down my cell phone number. If you see this girl here the next time, could you please drop me a call and let me know?"

The tea man was a sympathetic guy. Now the romantic winds were blowing in his heart too. He liked Hakan, he thought he was a sincere and nice boy. "Don't worry, son" he said, "if she comes again, I will learn her name and even her phone number. And I will definitely let you know."

Hakan noted down the tea man's phone number as "Tea-maker Uncle". He left the place and walked down to his car. He waved at the tea man looking behind him and started to struggle an inner feeling from the moment the car moved on. Now he wanted to see the girl again more than everything. Istanbul was a big town. His wish to meet the girl was even greater than Istanbul.

He arrived home. It was a day he would rather be alone at home. Upon opening up the door he hears his elder sister's voice. And when he stepped in, his mother's voice echoed in his ears. Another day this family meeting would please him a lot, but now it was most unwelcome.

He hugged his family. The elder sister asked, "You returned early. So, you didn't complete your walk?" Hakan answered unwillingly. "Erol was busy. And I don't fancy walking all alone. I felt bored." The other sister replied. "If only you'd let me know before you went off. I could accompany you."

Hakan's answer was even more farfetched. "Maybe next time?" That moment, he figured. Maybe it would have been better to go with his younger sister. She was a social butterfly just like her husband. She liked to make new friends...

He was sure, his sister would have found a way of talking to the girl with the mountain bike. And learn everything about the girl within five minutes. Definitely! "Yes, you are right, sis. I wish I had let you know instead of walking alone" he blurted out. The younger sister was happy to hear that. How could she know about her brother's mind. Forty foxes walked in the labyrinth of his brain and their tails were getting knotted into an impossible Gordian knot...

He was fourteen years younger than his elder sister and ten years younger than his younger sister. According to what their mother told, their father wanted to have both sons and daughters, and so a year after their marriage their first child was a girl, four years later, another girl came in. Their mother promised the third one would be a boy. But for ten years, nothing happened. Finally they visited the doctor and he told the magic word. Thus came Hakan to this round planet called earth.

Neither Hakan nor his sisters found out about the magic word, but Hakan liked his sisters a lot. They were good friends. Especially with the elder sister. And despite the age difference. They exchanged bad jokes, which cracked up the entire family. His sister would proudly tell that she fed him and replaced his pampers. Hakan would turn to his brother-in-law and ask how he could stand the elder sister.

They told Hakan was born through a difficult labor and survived a life threatening complication. Her mother was forty when he was born. Maybe this was a very advanced age at that time. And he conceived only to keep her promise. However, the father had given up the idea of a male child long time ago. "We have the sweetest girls of the world," he said. "Maybe we will have grandsons."

But the mother was stubborn, and wanted to keep the third baby no matter. It could have been a baby girl as well, but it wasn't and there was a cheerful air at home upon the good news. The elder sister was a 14 years old teenager and she wanted to take care of the baby. The younger sister was ten and she was a mischievous little sweetheart. So they were looking forward to their little prince.

So, Hakan was grown at home by three loving females. The only distant person was his father.

Hakan said he was tired and went up to his room without talking too much. And he did not leave until late in the evening. Afterwards he met Erol to go to the cinema. He didn't mention Erol about the girl, which surprised him too. Erol was one of his best friends. On Sunday, he was in the Belgrad Forest again. He had thought about the girl with the mountain bike all through the week. First he stopped by at the tea-man's coffee shop. The old man recognized Hakan at a glance and mentioned that the girl had not come. How was she? Was her knee well? Maybe she was just a guest in Istanbul. And at the end of her visit, she simply went back home. There were millions of possiblities and each and every one wringed Hakan's heart. Next week a new employee started at the architecture bureau where Hakan worked. This was a pretty, petite girl and apparently she liked Hakan, but he did have thoughts for the girl with the mountain bike only.

One Sunday he drove off to the forest again. The tea man was sympathetic for Hakan. "Listen son, you are really in love with this girl. They call this a blind love. Son't worry. Just wait. God will let you encounter this girl sooner or later. Just don't worry so much." Hakan listened half-heartedly. Blind love and so on. This was nonsensical. It was his fault to have lost the girl without even being able to meet her properly. They had met several times in the forest and...

He could not even say, "Hello, would you like to drink a tea here with me?" He grumbled, "Hakan, you useless..."

What could the girl say? "I don't want to drink tea. Please don't disturb me. Goodbye." And he would have said, "Ok then, farewell." End of the issue.

While leaving the forest, he promised himself. He was going to mingle with the new girl at the office. He would stare at her, flirt with her whenever possible.

At home, he found his family at the dinner table. He was happy about it. He sat down happily. In a few minutes, annoying sentences started to fly up in the air. One of his father's childhood friends was going to celebrate his silver jubilee in a hotel, with a lavish party. He insisted all the family to come over. Hakan should come too. His father's old friend, insisted that he definitely wants to see Hakan along. But Hakan did not like people he didn't know, nor did he enjoy lavish parties.

He asked shyly: "Is it OK if I do not come, dad?" His father answered patiently, "Why not, son, you would be entertained. And my friend is in the construction business. It will be good for you if you know him. Maybe your company would get a project from his company one day. Since he wanted to get to know you in particular..." Hakan added nervously, "Dad, we have a lot of projects. We do not ask for any favours." Now his father was annoyed about this tone. "I really want you to come along. If you come, I will be very happy. İf you don't this will be gross. That's what I will say. Good appetite to everyone." He said and left the table.

Hakan was stunned. For thirty seconds he felt dizzy.

Then he asked his mother, "Mom, do you see how my father reacted?"

"What's wrong with it, son?"

"What more! He is emotional-blackmailing me. He will be very happy if I come, and it will be gross if I don't. What does this mean now?"

The sisters were mute. On one hand, their parents, on the other hand, their little prince. What could they say? Hakan did not have a second chance. He spent the next two sundays in the forest. He waited in wain for the girl. The tea man was regretting not having learned the girl's name or phone number. Hakan's inner voice told him not to give up. It was already one month. His was a vain dream! How could he find her in this giant city? And if he did, what would happen next? He kept on asking himself these. Meanwhile, the unwelcome day finally arrived. This the Party day. His mother went to the hairdresser, his father had an awesome shave at the barber. Hakan dressed up unwillingly. He was grumpy, but his father preferred to ignore his son's bad mood.

They met with his sisters and their husbands in front of the hotel. They went together to the lobby, and then to the hall. When advancing towards the guest hall, Hakan's heart started to pound. Was it the girl with the mountain bike he was seeing? Yes! She was shining among all the guests. Next, there was an aged man and a woman accepting congratulations. She was between them. Hakan's father was walking in front, Hakan and the others followed him. The elderly couple might be the girl's parents. This was such an unexpected miracle. The entire hall disappeared from Hakan's eyes. Now there was only the girl with the mountain bike.

"It's you!" he told the girl. And she answered, excited. "Yes, you were walking in the forest."

"How is your knee, could you recover well?"

"Yes," said the girl, "Yesterday I had an x-ray, it's totally recovered now."

"I wanted so badly to find you back."

"Yes, I wanted to find you too."

"That would be so nice to drink a tea with you in that beautiful coffee house."

"Yes, there would be nothing better for me now."

Hakan shook when his mother tapped on his shoulder slowly. He felt the long line of people waiting for him to end the conversation. "See you," said Hakan. "See you," said the girl. Hakan looked at his father. Their eyes crossed and the father vaguely smiled. A waiter took them to their table. Everybody had overheard their conversation! So, the two met before. They had no idea where they had met. But it was apparent that they enjoyed the situation. The younger sister couldn't curb her curiosity, "Hakan, what's your friend's name?"

Hakan tried to come back to Earth. "Her name? Her name is... her name... The girl with the mountain bike!"

The elder sister's husband said: "It is rather uncommon for a name, but sounds nice." Everybody laughed.

Two weeks later...

One evening, Hakan's father and the girl's father met at a hotel bar after work. Hakan's father was saying, "I can't believe this, How could that happen?" And the girl's father replied: "Do you remember, we had told each other that our children should marry if we have one son and a daughter."

Hakan's father: "I remember it well. This used to be a custom in Anatolia. How could you think of letting the two meet at an event?"

The girl's father: "She loves biking. She saw that mountain bike ad on the newspaper and..."

Hakan's father: "And they met! They would probably never imagine that we set this up."

The girl's father: "Don't ever mention it! If they knew, they would be sore at us. They shall never find out."

Hakan's father: "I won't even tell my wife about it. She would tell her daughters and they would relate the whole story to their friends, and then..."

The girl's father: "If my wife knew about it, she would tell it to her mother, and then the entire world would hear about it."

Hakan's father: "Come on! To our secret!"

The girl's father: "And to the happiness created by our secret!"

And both: "To our kids!"

Belgrad Forest...

The tea man at the forest received a letter while cleaning his garden. He opened up the letter excitedly and started to read...

Dear Uncle,

If you remember, I had fallen off the bike. My knee bled and it was covered with dirt. I was scared! You had dressed my wound. Later, I visited the doctor, who found your dressing very successful. Thank you.

Dear Uncle,

I am engaged with Hakan, whom you apparently know. Ours was a "Blind love" you said! It's true. I was unconsciously waiting for him all the time. I found out about it later. We will come with Hakan to present you our invitation when our wedding date is set.

Dear Uncle,

I kiss your hands with respect and affection. Take good care and do not forget us.

The Girl with the Mountain Bike.

The tea man read the letter several times. Everytime he read, his eyes were getting full of tears and he tried to dry them with his big handkerchief. He got up and placed a casette into the tape recorder. Now with the sound of music his shoulders started to move. His feet shivered. He was a man from the Black Sea. He could not stop himself anymore.

The passerbys and those who jog were indeed curious about why the old man was dancing like a lunatic.

If they had asked, they would have found out about the story of the Girl with the Mountain Bike and the Little Prince.

AZİZ NESİN:
"FOR ME, HUMOUR IS ONE OF THE MOST SERIOUS ISSUES"

The person who told this, is an ordinarius of laughing. Namely Master Aziz Nesin, whom we should study with care.

What is not in humour? Every subtelty searched in the thought will be found in humour. If only it was made in the hands of a master... Societies fond of humour take ideas, add them jokes, pleasantry and art and offer them to the reader. While we read or we remember, we laugh and we smile. If one objective of humour is to make one smile, the other one is to make one think. Laughing is an abstract -not real- non-tangible -designed in the mind- medicine. I do not remember who told it anymore, but isn't that correct?

Laugh, so that the entire world laughs with you. Because if you cry, you cry alone. Bernard Shaw tells about laughing (Şakir Eczacıbaşı – Gülen Düşünceler / Remzi Kitabevi) and he says:

Don't make me laugh,
For laughing melts off many rightful anger
It forgives many sins
And it saves the world
From many murders

Why is he saying, "Don't make me laugh"... He might be upset at someone. Maybe at the audience booing him. Let me tell you the story. Sorry if you have already heard of it.

A play of Bernard Shaw is being staged in London. A great applause comes at the end. They invite Shaw to the stage. While the applause continues, a voice, suppressing all voices says "Boooo!" The applauders are surprised. The applauses slowly die off. The boo is going on with all its might. Bernard Shaw looks at the booing person from the stage and says: "My friend, we are of the same opinion, but what can we do against all this crowd?" Is there a more elegant way of putting an impertinent audience to his place?

When we talk about humour we can definitely not ignore caricature. Caricature is, as the old people say an "integral part" of humour. Every Wednesday, I take a look at İzel Rozental's corner on the first pace of the Şalom Newspaper, "The End of the Tunnel". Sometimes the end of the tunnel takes me to a trip at the depths of thought. Then I meet the "Mosotros Family" of Irvin Mandel in one of the inner pages. In these family members I find traces of our society. I also try to follow the caricatures in the newspapers that I read.

I think especially caricatures without words are real mental exercises. Thought invites thought. If I do not write down what springs to my mind, I will feel guilty. There should be a continuous humour corner in daily or weekly newspapers, monthly or trimestrial magazines. These corners should offer a space to topics outside religion, sex and politics (to be discussed). Let's try to imagine. A single page humour corner on the solemn Time, Newsweek, The Economics, Fortune or similar magazines.

Would it fit? Definitely, moreover the print runs would increase.

Solemnity is a photocopy of seriousness. Humour is the sweetener, and sometimes the salt and pepper of moderate behavior. Our old and grumpy world needs to laugh. More than everything... Such that the secret of success is hidden on the relaxation of facial muscles.

A TALE:
THE WIND AND THE SUN

Let me tell you the tale first, then we shall discuss its morale...

The wind and the sun compete all the time about which one is stronger. The wind would say, "If I blow, I destroy everything in front of me, I become the nasty west wind, the boreas, the mistral, the tsunami, I pitilessly crash everything that stands in front of me." And upon hearing this, the Sun would stand up. "I," it would say, "I am the biggest power on universe, I am a great celestial object, I spread warmth, I spread light."

At the end, they present themselves to the Great Creator of the Universe. "God, tell us, which one of us is stronger?" The greatest power smiled, "Let's make a test. Whomever is more successful shall be stronger." He said. "Allright," say the Sun and the Wind, "let's have the test."

God brings them in front of a window. "This is the window that opens up to our world. You see that man walking in that country, that town, that road. He's wearing a coat. We will set a time limit. Within this time, you shall take the coat off him, but without wounding or killing him."

They toss a coin and the wind starts to blow. When the man felt the wind, he held on to his coat. The wind speeded, the man hugged a tree. The wind uprooted the tree and the man sought refuge behind the walls of a building. The wind destroyed the buiding. The man rolled his arms around his coat. He was rolling on the way the wind took him. But the time was over and it was the Sun's turn now. The Sun sent its rays towards the man. Upon seeing that the wind has stopped and the sun appeared, the man got up and tidied his outfit. When the weather became a bit warmer, he took off his coat and took it to his arm, started to whistle a song and walk.

Dear readers, I remember the person who told me this tale very well. There was the Tifdruk Matbaacılık Şirketi in Istanbul Topkapı, on the Davutpaşa Avenue some 30, 40 years ago. Sometimes I chatter briefly with their chief accountant. I feel disappointed now as I did not keep his name in my memory.

When I heard the tale, I told myself, "So what?" But as years passed, I started to grasp the message of the tale. I did not need much time to see that violence would always lose in the family or in business relations. It is a great expression, "Sow the wind and reap the whirlwind" and it hosts so many memories of mine approving my thesis.

For example, there were violent tensions on the relations between workers and employers in years 1970-1980. Time to time people preferred to be the wind. But the country saw great harm. Then there was a revolution. On the spectrum from social relations to economic reasons, the violence is represented by the wind and tolerance and understanding, by the sun. Such that in politics, anger and rage are represented by a hawk and those who want peace are represented by a dove.

And the world politics is signifying these two birds. For example, they resemble Bush to a hawk. And Bill Clinton is depicted like a dove. Only time will show us which one is Barack Obama's favourite costume...

LAUGHTER AND CHOPS

Apparently, one laughter is worth two chops. It's the specialists who say it. I'm just the mediator.

This is a delicious proposal-hypothesis for young ladies and middle aged guys to eat less and get rid of extra pounds... Laugh a lot, but stay away from food. Your psychological condition will replace food anyway. If it is completely true, humour and comedy has it all and too bad for food sellers. And alas, among all these important issues, some of us are doomed to stay moody.

Talking about important issues, what is an important issue?

For example, it is a matter of curiosity to know where our god is, after the world was created by god by rules other than set by Darwin. Here is an important one. Now let's digress...

In a little village lived a chief and he had two little sons, aged five and six. These two had a role in almost all the mischief happening in the village. Under every malice they appeared. Village people were sick and tired of them, but since they were the cihef's sons, no one could react.

One day a young and fresh imam came to the village. The chief liked this serious looking young man very much and asked him for a favor: "My kids do not fear anything. If they had fear of God they would behave and the village people would take a breath. Would you talk to them?" The imam accepts with all his heart and tells the chied to send the younger one first, and the next day, the older one, that he would speak to them accordingly.

The younger son arrives at the imam's place. In fact, he was planning with his elder brother how to chase the imam out of the village. So the imam and the boy sit against each other. The imam asks with a serious voice: "Where is God?" The boy is surprised. He looks in front of him, without an answer. Now the imam repeats shouting. "Tell me, son! Where is the God?" The boy looked down. No answer. So the imam raised his voice once more. "So your good for nothing brother doesn't know where God is?"

The imam pulls the boy's ear, and the boy sends a kick to his belly. Crumbled in pain, the imam leaves the kid's ear. Running, the boy arrives home and goes straight to his brother's room. And short of breath, he says: "Now we are doomed. God is lost, he is nowhere to be found. And they think it's our job!"

My father, now deceased, mumbled "Where is God?" while listening to the French Radio during WW2. I was 8 or 9. If I could tell this story to him, maybe he would smile a bit.

DO YOU LIKE POETRY?

Life is poetry
Let's know it like this
Let's read its verses
Happily together

Dear readers, would you like to make a potpourri of poetry today? I would like to offer you some verses I felt intense while writing.

First of all, a short excerpt from my play "The Awakening".

The 13 years old Ayla leans down while watching the sea, so much that she loses her balance and falls into the sea. Her father dives into the water and saves his daughter but dies of exhaustion. Ayla feels responsible for his death and suffers from remorse. So she complains:

My poor father,
The dearest hero of my childhood days
A Bonanza, a Superman
Your daughter killed you, unwillingly, unknowingly
They call it childhood, at the age of thirteen,
Without thinking where it all would arrive
I want to cry, with all my might, with all my tears,
Hidden in my orbits, my tears, Get out of your deep hideaway
Let all bitterness in me flow away with you
And bad memories.

Another excerpt of the same play. The surgeon calls upon God before starting a critical operation;

O God, mighty God,

I pray to you before every operation,
I consult thee for
My desire to keep alive
The heart you have created, the soul you granted.
Give power to my hands, my fingers holding a scalpel,
Direct me, my mind and my skills
To make happy, this unfortunate soul,
Here I am begging you.
Death is nature's law
The end of life, maybe bitter maybe sweet
Whatever it is, my duty bestowed, Is to make people live
To offer a bunch of flowers
To beauty and to life

And here are four verses of a long poetry I had written back in 1955...

We simple people, we are neither left, nor right
Our prime pleasure, is to be a vagabond
And we are ignorants, we do not speak French
Never mind, it only counts not to starve.
Socialite? Mille pardon, who is this?
A fortunate name for the smart rich?
Please pay attention, do not disdain
Is it a sweet tit for tat for the sweet democracy
Wait Yakup, none of your business actually
Care about your joy in this heavenly earth
Let fake attitude race with dandyness
Give up on everything, just don't be an ass.

Half a century passed ever since. But there are texts which do not lose actuality. There's no harm in remembering them time to time.

MEMORIES, DREAMS OF WHICH, ARE WORTH A WHOLE WORLD

An article written by a columnist sometimes takes the reader to the past. This happened to me. I can show Bekir Coşkun's article "We Are Made of Ink and Paper" in Hürriyet newspaper.

While ingesting the lines one by one, some images came to life in my mind. I am the representative of the Gebr. Schmidt GmbH Printing Inks Factory. After a French company, it is the second one in Europe in the factory industry. In 1980's, it had two thousand workers. I had started to represent them in Turkey in year 1967. I carried out this duty for 35 years.

One of their primary objectives was to ensure that one of the major newspapers in Turkey, like Hürriyet gets printed with their ink. I met with Fatih Bey, who was the purchasing manager at Hürriyet back then. "I know the factory. If the quality and price fits, we will purchase from you" he said. One month later, we were at the printing facilities of Hürriyet with samples in our hands. Next to me was the export manager of the Germans, Horst König.

It was past midnight. The inks were poured into the feeders of the giant machines and the rotatives started to move. Then a rather slim guy came in. Workers were all eyes and ears. I asked the technical responsible of Hürriyet standing next to me. "Who came?" He replied on the spot. "Haldun Simavi Bey." Haldun Bey passed by, he saluted us but did not stop to talk.

I was excited. I asked the guy next to me, "Does Haldun Bey know about technics and printing?" I will never forget the answer I have received. "If one day the Hurriyet workers strike, Haldun Bey could come in and print the newspaper all alone."

I cannot tell the admiration I had for the newspaper's boss. I heard later on that the print quality pleased Haldun Bey a lot. The Germans were determined to receive an order from Hürriyet. The price was discounted a lot compared to all local and international competitors and we received an order of around a hundred tons. The rest of the story developed like this: Local inkmakers could not face losing a customer like Hurriyet Newspaper and they discounted their price to gain their sweetheart back.

Fatih Ediboğlu was an examplary gentleman. He was honest and knowledgeable. When I heard that he was the son of Baki Süha Ediboğlu, I remembered some of the radio programs I liked so much to listen to in Ankara and İstanbul.

I have a memory with Nezih Demirkent. We met in one of the little busses making a ring between buildings at the Drupa Fair in Düsseldorf and we sat side by side. He was a magnanimous person. He slapped his big hand to his knee and said, "Tell these Germans to discount their price without tricking with their quality, so that we buy ink from you too." May he rest in peace.

The smell of screen printing, typo, offset, flexigraphy and tiefdruck printing houses is more frangant for me than the best known French perfumes.

WHAT IS ART?

It is a person's production of a work, with the aim of gaining his own or other people's appreciation. This work can be a painting, a sculpture, a ceramic piece, a music piece, a poetry or a prose. You might call this definition superficial. But then you will need to complete it. A work of art shoud create a sense of beauty on its viewer... and on the thoughts as well.

If an appreciation by himself is the issue, we may say that art is for the sake of art. For another person or society, the aim can be "Art for the sake of people". The discussion whether art should be for the sake of art or people goes a long way. Probably, the person to decide should be the artist himself.

Whatever the artist intended, let it be!

The artist should be on the pursuit of novelties as well. Then he would surpass himself. Can we not say this? Art is for the sake of art and society at the same time. Is that not more realistic? A product of art is born from the artist's heart and mind. Every artwork which received value and interest from human beings consists of a combination of heart and mind.

A product making the brain work fast can be very valuable, but can we call it art?

In the same way, a product which just touches our heart may be applauded, but is it a work of art? I am doubtful. If a work of art can melt thought and feeling within one pot, then it deserves to be called an artwork. When I was looking at the works exposed by painting and sculpture masters in New York, Art Expo Fair thisd week, such were my thoughts.

Almelek Art Gallery joined the fair with the works of Moiz Benezra. Just like a bee visiting every flower, my eyes were running from one production at the stand to another.

Suddenly, I paused with a very familiar sound of music.

Now it was my ears' turn to perceive and to enjoy. The sound came from a cell phone. It was actually a Song by Tarkan which shed around joy.

The phone's owner was searching for the device in panic in order to mute it. I secretly wished he could not find it. I wanted to hear it once more and once more.

It was as if it became one with people everywhere and under all conditions.

This connection is not with music alone. Now it spread to painting and sculpture. Now an industrial company could produce a device with a painting of Picasso on it.

Not only the rich, but also people with modest budgets are able to enjoy visual arts now, with screen posters and litographies they ornamented their walls with. One was using a Shakespeare sonnet while looking for a market for his product.

In some countries, industrial enterprises now have the obligation of sparing 1-2% of their budget to artistic activities. My best respect and affection to those who add beauty to beauties.

LAUGHING THOUGHTS

Let's lend an ear to what the great British humourist George Bernard Shaw says. Let's see what he says in his pay called Jeanne d'Arc: "When the English want to invade a country to find new markets for their products, they send there missionaries. (As known, missionaries are religious men appointed to disseminate their religion) Missionaries impose a suppressive regime to christianize the people. People oppose to this, harrass the missionaries and sometimes kill them. Then the English invade those lands under the pretext of protecting the missionaries.

How do they do it? Very easy. They spread the news that these lands are a gift of God for the English. Indeed, one should protect the God's gift well. It is no longer a matter of discussion to whom the great empire of the seas belongs. They destroy those who oppose them and fare to the other end of the world."

Gerogre Bernard Shaw is an Englishman. Sorry, an Irishman. However, he does not hesitate to criticize the country he is a citizen of in the harshest way. In "The Man of Destiny" he chastises the English: "There is no good or evil the English are incapable of doing; but you cannot see an English doing something wrong. Everything he does is for the sake of a principle. He fights you because of the patriotism principle. He robs you because of the trade principle. He turns you into a slave because of the empire principle. He crushes you because of the bravery principle. He supports his kind because of the loyalty principle and he beheads him because of the republic principle."

Are the English a virtuous society? According to Shaw, they will readily side with virtue if it doesn't bring them a monetary or intellectual responsibility. In another country, a writer expressing such opinions about the country in which he was born and bred may run into trouble, but a society as open to self-criticism as the English are hard to find on this globe.

Quite on the opposite, the English did not delay in showing the greatest respect and affection they could show to Shaw. What is criticism? It is an examination. It is a judgement to find, show and tell the right or wrong, the beautiful or ugly, the good or bad sides. There should be no place for malevolence in this judgement and no prejudices shall prevail

That's why George Bernard Shaw was read and applaused in the main countries of the world and especially in Britain, for the 94 years that he lived. More than half of the 53 plays that he has written are being brought to the world stages. In his plays he was sarcastic about poverty, marriage relations, prostitution, vain glories, class distinctions. He made laugh and think at the same time.

"If I did not manage to make laugh, they would have crucified me." This preoccupation of Shaw proves his mastery in making think while making laugh.

"Laughing Ideas" is the name of the book dear Şakir Eczacıbaşı has written over Shaw. The book's preface starts like this: "London shook with a news in the morning of November 2, 1950: Bernard Shaw died..."By losing such a genius, the world shook as well. However, we can repeat what Shaw told for William Morris for Shaw himself as well: "One loses people like Bernard Shaw only by his own death, not when he dies."

DOVES AND HAWKS

Here is a superb sentence! "What have we not done for this land... Some of us died and some of us held a speech."

It is a slap in the face, with a pinch of humour.

It is possible to divide people into several categories: Beautiful, ugly, smart, stupid, bonehead, shrewd, and so on. We could add yet another category. Those who die for a cause, for example for their country. Those who, for the same cause, hold a speech or talk through their hat. If we would dig deeper into the meaning of this sentence, what else would come out!

Some say, "it is a duty, it is your debt to the society" and fight, suffer, shoulder all the pain with the inner knowledge that he stands all this for the survival of the next generations. Some other does not want to mingle, for danger is not something acceptable to his taste. He has to steer away from those that happen to the other, but he wants to show up as well.

So what does he do? He produces big words. For example: "These lands are holy, they are not to be given up!" he says. When it comes to words, he is the big hero. He says let's fight, but he does not move a finger. Usually, he is not even living in that land. These people talk on, in the comfort of belonging to the same religion.

When he is told to go to that land and live there, which answer will he give? He will blow a lot of smoke. His excuses are ready. His funniest appearance is that he also looks convinced with the excuses he brings up.

But, will he ever make an effort? No way!

Fighting is an expensive social disaster. Every year, the money spent for wars reaches a trillion dollars. This incredible sum is usually paid by smaller countries. That's why small countries have a hard time growing. Those who want war or who find war necessary have to contribute for it. Otherwise this should be called a cheap, theatrical heroism.

Peace should not mean peace at any cost. To attain peace, there should be an equilibrium between what is given up and what is gained. Otherwise, this will not be peace, but the glory of one party and the disaster of the other.

Making peace is much harder than making war, for it requires quite a strong mind and intelligence, a solid sense of logic and a contemporary understanding of future. It requires a sensitive soul, but also a strong will and patience. Is it not a nobler approach to foster doves rather than having a sympathy for hawks?

Note: Doves represent peace, while hawks represent war.

LEBLEBİ

Leblebici kavura/Dumanını savura
Bili bili bili bili/Leblebiciii
*Let the leblebi man roast/and blow its smoke
Bili bili bili bili/ here's the leblebi man

A group of middle aged people consisting of relatives, friends and neighbours were dancing together. Some others mumbled the song. Some others interpreted a belly dance by shaking their tummy. There stood baskets at the table against the wall. In each of them, a different leblebi product. Salt free leblebi, salty leblebi, mastika leblebi, soy leblebi, clover leblebi, fruity leblebi, chocolate leblebi, broken leblebi....

The dancers dove their hand into the baskets with short intervals and dropped a few leblebis into their mouths. Who knows, maybe they hoped to gain the lost energy back. What a snack leblebi is, you eat it, yet you compose songs for it and moreover you produce expressions for it! We give our national snack a big hail.

Leblebi is made of chickpeas. After being peeled off, chickpeas are roasted. Some inventions bring flavour to this craft. For example, covering leblebis with soymeal. They say it has zero cholesterole. Salt-free leblebi is an ideal food for those who want to slim or remain in shape. I have heard dieticians recommending salt-free leblebi. It even helps to quit smoking.

We read on the newspaper that in Serinhisar district of Denizli, they organized last July the sixth "Leblebi and Culture

Festival". The governor of Denizli emphasized during his speech that leblebi should finally become an export product and the world should taste this snack of ours. There's a plate on my table and it is full with yellow, salt-free leblebis. While enjoying them, I try to remember some of our sayings about this snack, which is the best friend of rakı.

An example: a strong personality is called an "iron leblebi".

Friends, be fair and don't get surprised

Don't think we'd ever get sick as a *demir leblebi*.

Our prime minister has a crush for leblebi. We learned it from one of Hakkı Devrim's articles. You surely know Hakkı Devrim. He writes at Radikal. Moreover, he is the usual guest on TV programs. During TV shows he listens often and talks seldom, but whenever he talks he talks good.

In one of his speeches, our prime minister resembled our foreign debt to leblebi and snacks.

Maybe we should not mix politics into our leblebi but I think he is totally right. Touchy people are not only skittish about everything. They are also skittish about leblebi. If you are a businessman and if you have a secretary, you can tell her this: A good secretary is the one asking few questions. She would get the word "leblebi" before you start with "leb-".

Leblebi is the muse of songwriters and composers as well. Pasaporte Latino's casettes are sold out. Too bad. I would love to listen. Nazan Öncel's CD's keep on ornamenting music shops. I would like to end my article this week by offering a few lines by her:

Every bite we took, we paid it back
And we learned, how to pay back
An iron leblebi, neither to be eaten, not to be swallowed
And some things maybe are not to be back.

A NON-FIGURATIVE STORY

One of our statesmen who is retired now and who gained the society's appreciation with his paintings told in front of one of Picasso's paintings: "What's so special about it, I can paint it too." He might be right, but we have to give this: Picasso thought about that painting before everybody else and contributed to the development of a new movement. So, what is so special about that painting? When observed, it does not recall naturalness, in other words the appearance. It is not descriptive. It does not copy the nature. It does not have a structure, offering what it sees like a photograph. It belongs to abstract art.

It is also possible to call abstract art non-figurative. A tree may not remind a tree. And the human face, when looked upon may offer another shape. Why? The artist's mind abstracts what he does while he is producing something from what he sees. Could this tendency in visual arts not be reflected upon prose? There is a plethora of examples.

I tried to create an example. Things that happened to a letter... The owner of the letter was fond of it. She did not want to leave it, that somebody else takes it. She was going to fight with all her might, do whatever it be so that this precious sheet of paper reminds by her side. She started to produce remedies.

A letter should be placed in an envelope and presented in this way. This was the style. However, she did not like traditions and wanted to live in her own way. She forgot to place the letter into the envelope. The next day, she remembered to place it into the envelope, but then she left the envelope on the table. The night came, it became dark, then the sun rose again. She remembered about the envelope, she placed it in her bag. Now she left the bag in the sofa. She got in the car and drove. She arrived to her friend's house. But what now, the bag was left at home!

She told herself she was sorry. It must have been a twist of fate. It wasn't her fault. She returned home, took the bag, placed it into the car. But then she forgot to get in the car. She was desperate. God does not want me and my letter to part, she figured, otherwise, why should it disappear from my mind in such a way?

She hopped in her car and the car drove. She found her friend. They hugged. She mentioned the letter. She said she was going, she asked her to send the letter but her friend was in a busy time then. So she didn't remember the letter. She was floating in a sea of thoughts. So she let go.

The man with gray hair arrived to the train station with slow steps. He asked the engineman of the waiting train, "Son, a letter was to be left for me, do you have it?" The machineman was a smart young man. He said, "No old chap. I don't have it."

The man with gray hair was sore about the word old chap. "Isn't that a bit impudent, the way you call me?" The young man, "What else should I have said and why is it impudent? Impudent is what happens under a blanket in the night. And it is definitely not the case here."

The old man thought while suppressing his anger. "The best answer to these people is silence."

Other trains were waiting at the station. The old man asked the same question on and on. No one asked him back "Who are you, why should a letter be left for you?" No one needed to ask. They didn't even take him seriously. So, was he not someone to be taken seriously?

He sat on one of the benches at the quay. He started to laugh. Only he knew what he was laughing at.

THE VOICE OF CIVILIZATION

I will host a guest at my corner this week. His name is
Beki L. Bahar. She is a playwright. She also collected her
memories in a book "From Legent to History, The Jews of
Ankara". She apparently loves poetry too. Let's read Beki's
lines aloud:

At the Bosphorus, in Ortaköy
Beki L. Bahar
A dilemma
A pursuit
An escape
A migration
A surge
Some found their fortune
And arrived to the Ottomans
Some remained to me and you
The seas are a well of secrets
The roads silent
Somewhere at the Bosphorus
In Ortaköy
When feet stepped on the land
The lips touched the ground
The soil was blessed in the name of the creator.
Thanks were given to Beyazıt Han,
A saint voice was heard
Azan
The shade of a cross reflecting freedom

The clock!
And the autumn started a psalm from the heart
The knot of fear
Untangled in plenitude
Ever since side by side
Three steps apart
Loving gazes
In the city of Istanbul
Azan,
Clock
And the autumn.

This poetry was read in the ceremony held for the environmental reRorganization of the Ortaköy square by the Mayor of Beşiktaş Ayfer Feray on April 26, 1992. I shall make an addition. The poetry is still hanging on a plate at an electricity pole. It is nice of the district of Beşiktaş to display it to the passerby.

Dear Readers,

One of the main reasons why I wanted to share this poetry with you is that it is contemporary, in other words, it bears the soul of the 21th century. There are three religious edifices in the Ortaköy square, three steps apart from each other. The mosque, the church and the synagogue. They smile at each other and to the people of Ortaköy and to Istanbul and to Turkey and to the World... And let's wish that the prayers raising from these three holy buildings form the base of a civilization the human beings are worthy of.

Amen, Amen...

THE PERFECT WEDDING

Dear Readers,

Last week I watched two plays in Vienna. One of them was "The Perfect Wedding" and the other "Beyond Therapy".

Let me offer you a short clarification. In Vienna, there are two theaters offering plays in English all the time. These are Vienna's English Theatre and the International Theatre. They both only interpret works in English. No translations take place in their program. Because a translated work may lose certain points and some meanings may change. The Viennese do not want to take such a risk. That's probably why the Art and Administrative Director of the theater Julia Schafranek says, "We only stage plays which are written in English."

Both of the plays I have seen were comedies. The viewers go to see the plays to laugh, but beyond spending a fine time, don't they return with something in their heart?

Let's take a quick look. Perfect Wedding. The dictionary gives the meaning of "perfect" as absolute, complete. Can there be a perfect wedding? Most of us survived a wedding. Did we not drop a brick? Whomever comes out and says "Ours was complete and perfect", shall be saluted in adoration.

Does the playwright Robin Hawdon think that way? Yes. My interpretation was in this way. In America and Britain the groom-to-be organizes an entertainment with other male friends. Girls are not admitted to this meeting. This is called a Bachelor's Party. What is the objective here? Marriage is an institution with a strong social side, requiring a lot of responsibility. The intent is to let the hell break loose and let the groom-to-be do whatever he wishes before going into this turmoil and so he shall drop his signature with a light heart the next day.

The play's main character Bill is someone we can call nice. He is 20 years old. He has a tendency to lean on wherever a pure wind blows. He is in love with a girl. Let's put a dot to this sentence. Maybe he thinks he is in love.

Warning to young people: Be careful! Which of your friends of the opposite sex are you fondest of? Don't fool yourselves. Otherwise you will look like Bill. Bill's first mistake was this. He made his bachelor's party at the same place where the wedding party was to be thrown next day. Are there no other hotels in London? What can I say? Probably a lack of experience...

Bill was totally drunk in his Bachelor's party. Completely and utterly drunk. He arrived to his room somehow placed his head to the pillow and fell into beautiful dreams. He woke up late the next day. And what did he see? There's a girl laying next to him. The girl sleeps tight. He shakes the girl and wakes her up to ask:

"Who are you?"

The girl looks at him in surprise and asks:

"Who are you?"

The kids are nice, there's no evil intentions in their hearts. I don't want to give any more spoilers. I have just one wish. Do you remember having watched this play in Istanbul? Could it have been staged in Profilo Center or in Beyoğlu? I think I remember it, maybe it is just a game of my mind.

Dear Readers,

The other play that I have seen in Vienna was "Beyond Therapy". I hope to share it with you another week.

Theater is life and life is a theater.

THE BARBER'S SHOP AT THE TOP OF THE SLOPE

Saturday, half day, Sunday, full day. These were his favourite days. They offered a time to stroll around and to get rid of the little thoughts in his mind. A great happiness lasting for one and a half day. The best was that this geographical voyage repeated itself four times a month. He thought often. God was a generous unknown.

He was 19 and considered the weekend as a valuable gift by the holy architect of the universe...

What had happened that week! He had worked at the company until Saturday noontime. In the afternoon he had met his friends. They were gone to the cinema. The movie was terrible, but no problem, their joy sufficed to overcome every annoyance. After eating at the pudding shop they visited every week, they would chat in the house of one of them, until the small hours of the morning. And the usual topic was without any doubt girls.

Sunday the next day passed in the same sweet way. The four friends went to Kilyos, to swim. When he had returned home, how nice it was to watch the starts from his window. He wondered what these shiny celestial objects were doing. While humans looked at them, maybe they were watching the creatures on earth. Who knows!

On the first work day of the week he woke up with his mother's warning. "Come on, be in a hurry, you will be late!" He jumped off the bed and washed his face in a hurry.

His boss would be angry with those who were late. Workers should be timely. He missed breakfast but could catch the bus. When he stepped from the main door of the company, his eye searched the clock on the wall. He was three minutes early. "Bravo" he murmured himself. "Glory is with us."

The first person he saluted in the company ws his boss. And the first words of his boss were, "What happened, your hair is too long and you haven't shaved for three days!"

He was stunned. And sorry. If he could look into the mirror for once during that precious weekend, he would have seen what was wrong. He knew that his boss was right in being angry; employees shouldn't come to the office like that. He sat by his desk. His heart was heavy. Suddenly, he remembered that there was a barber shop on the avenue next to the company. If he would go there during lunch break... People said it was an expensive place. A luxurious shop. He tried to guess. How much could that cost? Maybe fifty percent more expensive than his own barber. Can not be more.

When the hour hands showed twelve, he ran there. The shop was stunning. This was quite different from his usual barber. While he was being shaven, he was asked, "Would you like a shampoo? How about a friction?" And so on. He was embarassed to say no.

When the feast finally ended, he asked how much he owed. He could not believe what he heard. It had costed more than twice as much as he had guessed. Fortunately he had enough money. He paid it. Work for five and half days. Pay the barber more than your half-weekly pay. This was the cost of a probability. He returned to the company. His boss had immediately realized the difference. "Have you been to the barber?" he asked. Upon the positive answer, "Good boy!" he had said. He was all sunshine to have heard this answer.

At home, his mother said his hairdo was very nice. His father wondered whether he wanted to show off to a girl. His friends, with whom he met after dinner told him his new hairstyle sat well on him. One of them, a girl, told him he looked very handsome. But none of them asked him how much he had paid for the barber. He always thought that day had a lesson in itself.

But he had learned to look at life from the same perspective...

WELCOME

I saw him twenty minutes after he was born. He was sitting in the arms of the nurse, as if he wanted to have a place there. He no doubt needed to be protected.

I looked into his eyes carefully, it took a few minutes. He opened and closed his eyelids a few times. I cannot tell how much I liked this little movement. I felt I was becoming unified with him. I felt a melody from my heart went from me to embrace him.

He started to cry. He was wiggling his arms and legs all the time. What did he want to say? Was he hungry? When he was in his mother, he was sharing everything she ate. He was in a comfortable place, back then. But upon setting foot onto our world, the conditions changed. Now he was a personality. His eyes were proof of a personality.

The nurse kept on telling him things. Did he get what she was saying? That beautiful obstetrics nurse, she undressed the baby, held him from his ankles and lifted him up, he was upside down now and apparently uncomfortable. With a linen meter, she measured him. Then she laid him on a balance to find his weight. In the tub next to the balance, she washed the baby while murmuring a little song.

Then she dressed him back with great care, answering his little smilies with a smile. The little baby, who was not even an hour-old was telling his thankfulness to his caregiver with his cooing.

I was looking at him as if I was looking at an artwork. This description is most true. Wherever in the world it is born, isn't a baby an incredibly lovely work of art that the wonderful power that we call God has gifted to life and society? I want to be friends with him. Words are useless! We will make it with the language of heart.

Time walks, time runs, time flies. As years go by, he will climb the steps of learning and I will struggle in order not to get lost in the seas of ageing. In the meanwhile I will watch him growing up. Thanking that this sight is one of the biggest gifts that God has given to me.

What will I tell him, when he has grown up? I do not intend to give counsel. Counsels make those who give them unlovely and those who receive them, worried. No one chooses his parents, his country or his religion. The Holy Creator of the Universe gifts these to the person when he is born. I can only create an ideal human portrait with my thoughts and my words and gift it to him. One should become a world citizen. This is only fit to an intellectual of the 21th century.

Turkey is the country where we are born, where we grew up and where our ancestors lived for centuries. It is our identity. We should do our best to raise it up. Without hesitation, we should be respectful of our religion. We have to show the same respect to the believers of other religions.

How will the ideal person of my grandchild be? I am curious...

Can, welcome to our world, you have brought joy to our family.

LOVE

Love is a concept like music to our ears. But how to define this word that we all know well and use very often?

Am I making a guess when I say, that we know it well? On which data or intiuition is my guess based on? Where's the role of our mind in this? Is the main source of love mind or heart? When can we say, "I have fallen in love"? It is difficult to detect. Although it looks easy...

Let's make one such clarification! Love is the interest and desire one feels towards the opposite sex. It is a psychological and physical desire. Now the definition sits a bit better... If there is no physical desire, it is called a platonic love. Far away from sexuality, a love that feeds only with dreams. Floating in the world of dreams, without touching the beloved. It is not everybody's cup of tea.

And there are those who do not believe in love. For them, love is an invented concept. If you ask me, they are wrong. Sometimes religious men prefer the explanation, "Love is the expression of a divine gift on humans." In other words, love is the reflection of a universal beauty. Or its sight. The person, who is in love with the beautiful is in fact giving his heart to the beauty of the Holy Creator. Seeking divine love, and even adoration in the opposite sex brings the person to new worlds and unifies him with the greatest of the powers.

If we move out of the religious framework, is there anyone who wasn't struck with love because of someone from the opposite sex? Fortunately, such infatuations are temporal. We quickly come back. Otherwise, we may never know where our feelings may take us. We can be a king, or a clown...

They say marriage kills love. There are surely cases verifying this, but this is also possible; marriage can weaken or destroy love but it may enhance affection between a couple and increase mutual fondness and solidarity. So, what shall we say? May romantism miss. Stability is good enough for us.

Is there a difference between love an affection? A writer says, "Love is an empowered way of affection, which can go beyond logic". According to him, apparently there can be logic in love or not. If we move gradually, the first step is affection and the highest step is love. We can fall in love with something we admire. Some of us will be struck with a work of literature, some with a melody, some with a painting.

There is a sculpture of three women dancing in our Almelek Art Gallery and I cannot stop from looking at them in admiration. I can confess I am deeply in love with Shakespeare lines. I can claim listening to certain songs of Tarkan is an insatiable pleasure. We all have preferences.

A friend of mine was prising Taj Mahal. I am sure he is right. Loving and being loved, these are two of the greatest gifts given to us by the Great Architect of the Universe. To fall in love and to be fallen in love. May God not spare us from any of these beauties...

A SINGLE PHOTOGRAPH

Photography is one of my favourite arts. Around three weeks ago, I took a look at the website of Nuray Uysal (www.nurayuysal.com) . Today, I visited the site again. Especially in order to look at her interpretations of birth.

There are not many photographers who take photos of babies right after they are born. I remember, four years ago I had a grandchild. Twenty minutes after coming to our world, the nurse showed us our guest from behind the window. Then I had regretted not having a photographer by our side. Back then, making an attempt with a smartphone was probably not a good idea. Twenty minutes later, he was there, eyes shut, face and skin in wrinkles, all naked, little fists clamped, crying with a voice unexpected from his size, -creating such a hell. Fixing that moment on a piece of photo paper would be such a visual delight.

Last month I went to Vienna for four days. I visited a museum. One of the galleries was dedicated to photography. Thirty something works of various artists. Just one baby photo. One in thirty.

In Istanbul I visit exhibitions of Ara Güler, Ersin Alok, İzzet Keribar and many artists I could not recall the names of. I look at their books. These are valuable works. However, I could never meet interpretations showing the post-partum, the baby as the main hero and the mother right after labor. Without any doubt, it is also possible to think of it as an unfortunate coincidence.

I congratulate Nuray Uysal for the importance she attached to this subject. As a photograph fan, I wanted to share it. I tasted this art not only as a viewer but also as an interpreter and I loved it. As I was serving as a reserve officer in 1965 in Erzincan, I met photography for the first time. Together with my friend Müfit Alişan we developed the photos I had taken with my camera branded Retina, made in the WW1 years. Wherever Müfit is, I'm sure he feels his ears burning. He was a physics engineer and we had learned to develop films by reading books. And our efforts gave a positive result. Before our discharge, we had also opened an exhibition at the officers' club of Erzincan. All the high school students visited our exhibit. The praising words of the people caressed our ears.

Last week a photo dropped onto my e-mail. It was as if it interpreted the dawn. The sun was gone, but the light was still there. Redness reigned still at the horizon. Maybe the sun wasn't rising yet and the eye-caressing color was the morning light.

The sun salutes its viewers when it is rising and setting and it smiles us sincerely.

What I saw was so beautiful... And it was even more beautiful to be able to enjoy it. To see the sunrise and the sunset. Just like birth and death. Just like arriving and being about to go.

That single photograph comprised all of these.

NAZIM HİKMET

Nazım Hikmet had set his easel at the courtyard of the prison and he was painting. İbrahim, who was around 17, approached with hesitation. Their eyes met. Ibrahim blushed, "Poet Father," he said, "I like what you are painting. Could you teach it to me?"

Nazım Hikmet's face lightened and smiling, he said "If you want, I will indeed teach." Then his poet father taught his pupil İbrahim how to hold a brush, how to obtain colors by mixing paints, what is perspective, every day, step by step. While doing this, he was not stopping himself from giving the ambitious young boy lessons from life. In the prison, all prisoners called Nazım Hikmet as "poet father".

İbrahim Balaban was imprisoned at a very young age because of self-defence. When he was set free, he worked and years after he became one of the best painters of the country. He carried Nazım Hikmet in his heart, and he still does.

Who is Nazım Hikmet? A Turkish poet. Besides, a world poet. He was born in Thessaloniki in 1901. He studied in military schools. He worked as a teacher in Bolu. He went to Moscow in 1921. He studied in the Communist University of Eastern Workers. After remaining there for three years, he returned home. The poems he wrote were often litigated, but he was acquitted from most of them.

He was arrested from creating a secret organization between 1933-1938, from sediting the army and navy and he was sentenced to prison for 28 years. He was released in

1950, benefiting from the general Amnesty Law. Next year he traveled to Russia. In 1951, he was expatriated with the council of ministers' decision. He traveled a lot until his death. He read his poetry, he gave speeches in conferences. Besides literature, he produced notable works in cinema and theater as well. Between 1938-1965, his works were banned in Turkey.

During school years we were secretly reading his poetry and lending them to each other. After 1965, his canon was reviewed and published by large publishers. His poetry, which he collected in his book "Human Landscapes from my Country" were dedicated to his wife Hatice Piraye Pirayende. I hardly recommend him to all those who like free verse. Nazım hikmet lost his life on June 3rd, 1963 in Moscow.

I would like to end this article with a poem Ibrahim Balaban had written for his tutor, Nazım Hikmet.

"I have seen those who turn handcuffs into medals, and shackles into necklaces.../ And I have carried / I suffered it in with my lives...

Now I will make something of it: over shackles and cuffs / Here I tend a black curtain in front of you... My dreams are hieroglyphs / I palpated the darkness searching for myself before I met my poet father. My hands found him at first. And he placed me in his place.

I write this book for Him

O hear ye!

I write it for Him!"

I time to time meet and talk with Ibrahim Balaban, the painter. His love towards his tutor Nazım Hikmet is examplary. The subject of my next article will be Ibrahim Balaban.

NATURE IS SACRED

It is sacred because it was created by divine powers and gifted to animals. This is the religious explanation. Everything constituting the universe, everything we can see, tough, smell, taste and grasp, every object creates together the nature and becomes an inseparable part of it.

Unfortunately there are those who belittle or despise these inseparable parts. We call them "humans". Now all of them, for sure, but a great part of them. Nature has one funciton: To offer an environment of happiness. Is that not true?

I believe animals were created to taste and enjoy life. A contrary hypothesis would be underestimating the Great Architect of the Universe. This is a concept evolving since the formation of our world. Besides physics, chemistry, biology, astronomy and geology, another scientific discipline was established. Its main objective is to protect the nature from senseless human beings.

They called it ecology. In other words, environmental science. In Greek, ecology means the science of residence. Natural environments and their residence are so important that this science would like to keep humans away from any disasters happening to them. It would like to, but how successful will it be? We often hear on the newspapers, magazines and on the visual media. Nature is dying.

There's one point we should not keep out of eye. Nature doesn't die alone. It would drag life away as well. As far as I remember from an information I have read in the weekly

Time magazine, at the beginning of our century, there were 6.5 (six-and-a-half) billion human beings living on earth. Besides human beings, there are many other creatures, animals, plants as well... However they do not create any important harm to their environment. To put it into words, they live quite on their own. Unfortunately, the entire destruction, harm and endamagement are caused by the bipedal creature. The human being allows himself to damage the beauty we call nature.

To a certain extent. After a long time taking centuries, it is hoped that an extraordinary power would intervene and nature would be restored back into its initial status. For example, solar energy can come here as a power. According to what is said, if a very small part of this energy was to be stored in a nutshell, it could enlighten an entire district or let a cruise ship travel in the ocean for months...

There are so many things waiting to be invented.

Sir Isaac Newton found the gravity and human beings traveled into the space, they even visited the Moon. Einstein produced theories explaining the relation between mass and energy. One day, someone will come up with something preventing pollution before pollution destorys humankind.

Let's not sink into despair. Someone will. We are waiting.

HOLOCAUST

Other known meanings of Holocaust are: a catastrophe, a disaster, a tragedy. A shame of the human history. Its meaning in our language is genocide. The aim of Hitler and his gang was to destroy the Jews, blacks, Gypsies, homosexuals and the impaired, to invade all countries outside Germany and to subdue them under a Germanic hegomonia.

According to them, the Germans were the Aryan (noble, clean) race and other nations should have served the Germans. Was Hitler an intelligent, reasonable leader? Thinking about his deeds and his sayings it is difficult to present a positive answer to this question, but it could be said that he was a problem with a great oratory power.

He wanted to become a world leader. The Jews opposed. He had understood that he was not going to convince them. What he had done were an expression of retaliation.

He was cunning. As cunning as to be able to drag a lot of Germans behind him. It would be unjust to blame all the Germans because of what has happened. There were hundreds and thousands of oppositionals. Unfortunately, they were afraid to raise their voice and they were passivised with an apathy of "apres moi le déluge".

The Holocaust started on January 30, 1933. The date it ended is May 8th, 1945. It is a period of international shame, which lasted twelve years. On January 30th, 1933 the Nazis came to power. Adolf Hitler was elected as the Prime Minister. His first deed was to end democracy and to start a general boycott against all the Jews in the country.

When the President Paul von Hindenburg died in 1934, Hitler proclaimed himself Chancellor. Now he was the only governor of the country.

In 1935 he passed the Nuremberg laws from the parlament. Accordingly, only Germans and those who came from German blood were citizens. This made the Jewish people in the country into hematlos.

In 1936, throughout the Summer Olympics, all brochures, handouts, posters against Jews were taken down. When the Olympic Games were over, they were placed back. He was apparently kidding the other Euroepans.

In 1937, he announced his intentions during a secret conference. These were invading Europe and eliminating Jews from all branches of society.

In 1938, he invaded Austria. He was planning to destroy 190 000 Jews who were living there.

In 1939 He attacked Poland and started the World War II. With a declaration, he ordered all Jews to live in ghettos.

In 1940, the German armies invaded Norway, Denmark, Belgium, France and Holland in the same order. The Auschwitz concentration camp was opened.

In 1941 they entered Russia. They created special platoons in order to execute thousands of people.

In 1942 six death camps were established. That year, three million European Jews' lives ended in gas chambers.

In 1943, killings continued in a discipline and system.

In 1944, There were movements against Hitler in the German army as well. The invasions had weakened.

In 1945, the American, Russian, English and French armies hit the German forces in the lands they had invaded. The Germans surrendered unconditionally.

In 1948, the State of Israel was officially founded. Turkey is one of the first countries which recognized Israel.

MEPHISTO

Who is Mephisto? A symbol of evil? The hero of Faust, the work of the German philosopher Goethe? Devil himself? A personality who does not know what pity is, an incorporation of treachery? Or a poor creature in a glorious appearance, collecting all of this in one personality?

What is his name? The hero of the play! Hendrik Höfgen? Why would it not be Adolf Hitlef?

Mephisto is being staged at the Urban Theaters of our beautiful Istanbul. It was written by Klaus Mann (1906-1949), son of the Nobel Laureate Thomas Mann and the theater version was created by Ariane Mnouchkine (1936-).

The director and interpreter: Ragıp Yavuz. Twenty one actors are helping Ragıp Yavuz with all their heart. The completeness they have created is so real and so artistic... There is one side of the Urban Theaters I like very much. The responsible of each role is separate. They do not save on actors. This creates pomp and richness. It literally sats the viewer's eye. My words should not be considered as a criticism of the private theaters. I know how they struggle and I am aware that this is praiseworthy.

Some short notes about the play...

The stage opens in the year 1923 and curtains close in year 1934. What happened in between these years are of nature and quality that every society in the world should draw a lesson. The National Socialists did not come to power by force. It was the people's votes which brought them there.

But once they held the power, they suppressed everyone else. Dialogue ended and monologue remained.

When the society realized what was going on, "that ship had already sailed". Those who raise unjustly, by stepping on to others find themselves soon or late abandoned. And it is inevitable for them to roll down.

Let me end my article by offering you an excerpt of Ariane Mnouchkine's 2005 World Theater Day speech:

Help

Tehater, help me / I am asleep wake me up / I'm lost in the dark, show me the light / I am lazy, embarass me / I am tired get me up / I am indifferent hit me / I am scared encourage me / I am a monster turn me into a human!

ON READING

Dear Readers,

I spent the last three days of last week in Switzerland. When I was traveling from Zurich to Bern, I had quite an interesting observation. I wish to share it with you.

I had taken the 14:00 express train. I was sitting on one of the middle seats in the waggon. From where I was, I could easily see those in front and those behind.

Without hesitation I counted firs the front rows then the back rows. There were 43 persons. Most of them had a book or a newspaper in hand. I say most of them, because I counted them too. Wight persons, five men and three women. They were either looking outside from the window or they were buried in their thoughts, looking vaguely in front of them. I was going to visit a sticker printing house in Bern. It was a short trip of around one hour and ten minutes. I will talk about it in another article.

35 persons out of the 43 people in the waggon had preferred to make good use of their time reading. When we calculate it makes eighty-one per cent. Maybe the words good use will sound wrong to some of you. You can ask me, "How do you know whether what they read was valuable?" My answer would be this, whatever we read, we make good use of our time. Reading graphic novels, growing interest into Darwin's theory or being taken taken by an erotic story, whatever we do, reading is spending time for something good.

Let's create a hypothesis. If more than seventy percent of the people read something while waiting the population of that country gains right to build a Switzerland. Readers ask some writers, "What shall I read? Give me some recommendations" they say. And the writers offer them their preferences. I can give an example. In the Kanyon shopping mall in Levent, at the entrance of the D&R there are interesting recommendations the well-known writer Doğan Hızlan has selected for you. If you happen to go there, don't miss it.

In the last two months, I have read works which gave me great enjoyment. The theater plays of Arthur Miller, "Death of a Salesman" and "The Crucible". All of Miller's theater plays were published as books. Each and every one of them are as thrilling and valuable as the other. The theater plays of the Nobel laureate writer Harold Pinter "Birthday Party" and "Betrayal" are indispensables of those who are interested in the stage. Pinter's plays are also offered to readers.

If you say, "No, we prefer novels", I can propose you "Son Ada" by Zülfü Livaneli without any hesitation. If I were a doctor, I would note this on the prescriptions I would write for my patients; "The subject is up to you, start a book that you like and finish it in one month latest."

I don't think so. I am sure that person will say he feels much better after reading. According to the statistics, the Swiss society is among the healthiest in the world. Why could that be, what would you say?

LET'S WRITE A NOVEL

Dear Readers,

Among you there must be some who would like to write a novel. For some, it surpasses a desire and becomes an instinct. Why not? If some reached success in a similar area, why would we not? We can at least try. If we arrive somewhere, good, otherwise, it is always possible to retreat.

First step: It is to start. Bring it on!

Subject: There are thousands. You can actually pick up a subject the way you choose a watermelon at the fruit van. Then you will elaborate it into a novel, a story or a play. Those with a sensitive heart may turn into poetry.

What would be the fruit of our efforts? No one knows. It is also possible that the watermelon is tasteless. But , you can also climb up in the sky with your private jet like Harry Potter's writer. Let me relate you a story that I had heard. The writer of Harry Potter novels, the British J.K.Rowling is a monther with three kids, born in 1965. She writes her first book and sends it to a publisher. Refusal! Another publisher, refusal! Yet another publisher responses, "We don't have place for such nonsense". How gross! No intellectual should ever make such a vulgarism.

However the fourth publisher thinks they can earn billions of dollars with these stories. And they do it too. The books beat sales records. So, by the power of her pen, J.K. Rowling becomes the richest mother of the world.

We can call it an exception. But, could exceptions destroy rules? Enlighten today with tomorrow. Told by E.B. Browning.

If we want something so much to ensure continuity instead of leaving it as a whim, we should start it now, say those who are experienced in life. If we can start today, why should we wait for tomorrow? By living, we learn how short life is. But I think to write a novel, one should be first very patient. Probably for this reason, skizzing short stories is for some writers much more cheering. However, the financial income of novels seems to be better. Those with the highest chance of sale are first novels, than short stories, memoires, theater plays and finally poetry.

It starts to become a custom in our society to gift a book on birthdays. A gift which can stay at home and which can leave a trace in the human mind. And moreover: light enough not to open up a hole in the budget. Cheap, but valuable.

Let's return to the beginning of the article. After finishing to read this article, let's take a pen and write something on a paper. But there shall be no leaving the desk before one hour.

Isn't that entertaining?

A REAL STORY

This incident happened on October 14th, 1998 during an intercontinental flight.

There was a fancy white woman sitting next to a black man. The woman called the flight attendant and in an air humiliating her seatmate, she asked her seat to be changed, for she did not want to sit next to someone antipathetic to her. The flight attendant told her the entire flight was booked, but she was going to see whether there are any free seats in the first class.

Passengers who listened to the woman's talking were in awe and repulsion. Besides the woman's shamelessness, they could hardly believe that now she was going to fly first class. The poor man, who was no different from all the other people in the world was just keeping silent. The woman seemed pleased. She was not going to sit next to a black and she was going to fly first class.

In a few minutes the flight attendant returned and told the woman there was one free seat in the first class section. And she had received the captain pilot's permission, who confirmed that "no passanger should be obliged to sit next to a troublemaker."

The passangers who were listening to the flight attendant were even more annoyed now. And the woman felt triumphant. While she was attempting to get up, the flight attendant turned to the black guy and said: "Sir, would you please follow me so that I can take you to your new seat at the first class? Our captain is excusing himself on behalf of our company for the inconvenience you had to experience."

The passangers applauded the good reaction of the captain and the flight attendant. And the woman had received a lesson. While the black passanger followed the flight attendant, she was as timid as a mouse. This incident caused travel agencies and airline companies to adopt new measures. That year the captain pilot and the flight attendant were awarded for their examplary attitude.

In order not to encounter similar situations, people need to be educated. Managers who are aware of this have hung these words on the wall of their seminar room:

"People can forget what is told to them.

People can forget what is done to them.

But people never forget how they are made feel."

Note: My sincere thanks to Okşan and Jerry Yusufyan who sent this story as an e-mail from Canada.

IDEAS AND OPINIONS

This week we are hosting an important person in our corner. I will talk about a book which Albert Einstein had started to write in 1919. In the same year when Atatürk came to Samsun and took a step towards the War of Independence, what a German man of science and thought has reflected upon, sair or written should be considered important; even a parallel can be found between the world politics and Turkey's success.

Name of the book: Ideas and Opinions
Translated into Turkish by: Z. Elif Çakmak
Publisher: Arion Yayıncılık
The book is presented in four chapters.
Chapter 1: Ideas and Opinions
Chapter 2: On Politics, Government and Pacifism
Chapter 3: On the Jewish people
Chapter 4: On Germany

It is such a book that the reader ought to stop and think after each and every paragraph. Einstein explains Antisemitism, which is an anti-jewish sentiment by a tale, which I think is mythological. I parpahrase. The shepherd told the horse: You are the noblest creature on earth. You deserve to live a carefree life and if that treacherous stag did not exist, your rejoice would be full. However, he works hard to surpass you in quickness since his youth. Because he is faster, he reaches water channels faster than you. While he and his tribe are drinking, you and your foals are left to thirst. Stay with me!

My wiseness and my guidance will save you and your kind from this sorrowful and lowly situation."

The horse, blinded by the hatred and jelaousy he feels towards the stag, accepts the proposal. So he lowers his head to the reins of the shepherd. He loses his freedom and becomes the shepherd's slave. In this tale, while the horse represents a society and the shepherd a class or group desiring an absolute power over this society, the stag signifies the Jews. I can hear you saying: "Such an illogical tale. No creature can be as stupid as the horse in the tale."

Let's reflect on this. The thirsty horse was demoralized as he was seeing the quick stag running around. If you have not tasted this pain and anger, you would not understand the hatred and blindness which pushes the horse to be tempted by such a proposal. In our tale, the horse is an easy prey to provoke, because the previous difficulties he has experienced have prepared him for making this mistake.

A saying: "It is easy to give others counsel which seems correct and wise, it is difficult for one to act correctly and wisely."A genius thinker was dissecting the wound of centuries with one tale. This book is ideal for a thought exercise ad maybe even necessary for certain societies.

WARNING TO THE YEAR 2010

Dear Readers,

Usually every new year is welcomed with standard words. One makes wishes and prayers. What is written in New Year cards mean more or less the same.

It is not possible to say that 2009 was a good year for our world. Especially the economic outlook was rather grim. It was also called a crisis year. And newsdpapers kept on writing; military spendings have reached 1.5 trillion dollers in one year. Let's think about what can be done with this money within twelve months. A great decrease in the famine among African younglings could have been celebrated.

2010 stands at our door and waits to be greeted with pomp. No, this time we will not do it. On the opposite, we will warn it. We will tell it to watch its step. Otherwise, we will call it a persona non grata.

Warning to 2010

Health and normal life should walk along
If they miss their way, by accident
One should push them together, by their ears
Year two-thousand-ten shall have a lot of joy
Life is a garden of lovely flowers
A person there is just a thorn
Two-thousand-nine is a misadventure
Two-thousand-ten the hope at the horizon
Be careful two-thousand-ten, do not hurt us
If you lose the good way you are treacherous
Be a step of kindness in this vain world
Or if you are evil, leave us alone!

YUNUS EMRE

Yunus Emre is a minstrel, a folk poet. What is folk? I went through dictionnaries in order to find the right definition. There are different definitions. Each and every one of the human groups living in the same country but coming from different origins, the whole people living in a certain region or an environment, the whole of a country's citizens. The definitions go on but there's one thing in common: For example, sense of unity in feelings and thoughts. For example, liking the same things, fearing the same things, or suffering from the same things.

Yunus Emre lives in the people since 800 years. No one exactly knows where he was born or where he died. It is said that he has a tomb in at least ten locations in Anatolia. It is a proof of how much he is venerated.

One of the hypotheses is that he was born in Eskişehir in 1240. It is also probable that he met Mevlana in Konya and he was impressed by him. Yunus Emre knitted divine love and humanistic affection, love, existence and nonexistence, life and death like a lace in his poetry. Wherever he roamed, he told people about equality and peace. And while doing this, he used a pure, simple language.

He gave us some of the best examples of folk Turkish. The examples are so numerous that I could pick a random one. The parantheses are my interpretations.

Neither rejoice do I for your existence, nor do I complain about your absence

I content myself with your love, you are the one that I need

(Which heart is so attached to the beloved these days?)

My heart fell into this loving, Come and see what love has done of me

I have given my life to this struggle, Come and see what love has done of me

(One shouldn't fall in love, love is scary)

Knowledge is knowing knowledge, knowledge is knowing yourself

If you don't know your self, then what is all that reading for?

(Pronouncing these verses 800 years ago?)

Yunus Emre is one of the poets who will exist as long as the world exists. He tells about mind and types of believing. For him earth, water, fire and wind are unified with the human soul. Earth and water describe heaven. Fire and wind are the items of hell. According to Yunus Emre, there are four phases of knowledge. These are: 1-Rules of religion, 2-Rules of sect, 3-Knowledge reached by intuition and reading and finally 4-The secret of God. He tells this secret with one single line: "You are holier than the holiest, yet no one knows what you are."

Yunus Emre has adopted the Islamic mysticism as a philosophy and he interpreted it too. According to him the person is a part of God. This observation brings those created gradually to the unity of existence.

If they kill me, let them throw my ashes to the sky

Let my dust call you, you are the one I need

Let's have a look at the condition of the world! Chaos reigns everywhere. One lie builds upon another. The truth is warped for small political and economic gains... This person who was addressing to fellow humans eight hundred years ago, would be very sorry to see all this.

BENEFITS OF FORGETTING

One could say upon this title, "Are there any benefits of forgetting?" In some cases, yes.

Forgetting is a word that all of us know. Moreover, it is a word we fear. Truth is; forgetting is like hell to some. An annoying dream. However, some happy-go-lucky don't care.

What is forgetting? Keeping something no longer in mind. Or not remembering something anymore. There is a soft, benign kind of forgetting too. We say it like this: "It's on the tip of my tongue." The concept remains on the tip of the tongue, but does not get out of the mouth as a word. It shows its head but keeps its body hidden. For a pupil waiting for the exam, forgetting is a nightmare. The vengeance of forgetting -usually in old age- is bitter. It brings one to a confused state of mind.

Forgetting is a mental status having directly to do with the mind. Would one fall into a great delusion here? Foolish head, weary feet, they say. Here the foolish head is actually a forgetful mind. Otherwise, every head contains a mind. The important is the quality of mind. The relationship between the head and the feet entered the political literature as well but our topic is forgetting, so let's stick to it. Şalom's doors are closed to such nonsensical talk anyway.

The opposite of forgetting is not forgetting, or remembering. Remembering is also called, 'recalling.' Remembering is a work of the memory. So, remembering is a searched word, or a past event coming out of the memory and being put into words. Memory is a storage place. We store words, incidents and knowledge there. Having a strong memory does not mean "Being very intelligent". As a proof to our claim we can show the Bedouins playing chess while crossing the desert on camelback. They are masterful players who keep every move in mind, in the absence of a chessboard, a pen, or paper. However, intelligencewise, it is not always possible to say they surpass the average. Let the relation between intelligence and memory the topic of another article.

A thinker said: "Forgetting is one of the greatest gifts nature has given to us."

I think he is right. What would have happened otherwise? If we do not forget, we have to carry all unfortunate events in our head. And when we remember them time to time, we suffer. The benefits of forgetting probably surpass its harms. So, let's address to the title of this article; long live forgetting!

THE FUTURE OF BOOKS

The word "future" is often used together with the word "bright". For example, for someone we do not know well we can say "This young man will have a bright future". On the opposite, "This business has no future" means a negativity.

Years ago, an engineer who completed the textile faculty abroad wanted to produce paper outfits for women. And he made it. The only issue was what the dresses would turn into under the rain. He had realized an invention preventing transparency, in other words, it was impossible to see through the dress, but when it was soaked with water, would this papyrus mixture still be ironable? In those days, newspapers openly expressed their hopelessness by writing: "This occupation has no future."

Let's move to another topic here. So, what will be the future of books? Is there a danger? Possibly. I shall present you the two inventions waiting to be exposed very soon. One is enjoying the taste of making your own book, pretty much in the do-it-yourself style.

This production will be as such; the reader will chose the book he likes from a library or from the publisher. The book will be sent to a machine. By clicking to a button, he will receive the book copy, typed in the fonts he selected. Second: The book content will be turned into a chip. The chip will be connected to the internet and by one click, the font and text type will be selected by the reader. In both cases, what will bookstores be doing? Will publishers have much less to do than they have today? There might habe been sharp declines in book print runs with the invention of tv. Instead of reading books at home, people prefer now to zap a box that offers continuous images.

Thanks to terrible TV programs, books can keep on having an existence by us and by the entire world. If the TV programs were really good, then no one would be able to keep their eye off the remote control. One can also observe that computers are now competing with books, such that you can read a novel from the internet. However, sitting in your armchair and shuffling a book's pages is awhole different pleasure.

No need to lose hope. We can keep on reading and writing.

Note: For the corner dated 27.08.2008, I would like to thank the Cumhuriyet writer Turgay Fişekçi

ANTI PRO AND WHAT A PITY!

The prefix "anti" brings a negativity when placed in front of words. It means against. A plethora of words starting with anti are existent in encyclopedias. For example: Antibiotics. Something against living beings. This prefix has a spooky character in medicine and even in literature. Or maybe this is my personal thought.

The prefix "pro" is the antonym of "anti". It is also a prefix, but it doesn't sound half as harsh and scary as the other one. It produces compound words, giving them the meanings of in favour, in front, instead. The prefix pro doesn't have a hardness or sorrow in it. Or maybe it is my personal thought.

Antisemitism is also a word produced with the prefix anti. It means Against Jews. To add a pinch of humour to this article, Antisemitism, What a Pity! Would be more appropriate. Why "What a pity"? Because it describes an act of pity. To whom? To the person who is an antisemitist. What a pity! To foster sentiments of loath and antipathy towards another one does the biggest harm to the one bearing those sentiments. A bad temper harms its possessor most.

The word antisemitism did hurt me until last week. I was asking myself why some people do not like Jews. I think by pondering on it, I have reached an answer. Most of the people are not in the need of loving, but they want to un-love. It is not of importance who is not loved, as long as the negative sentiment is felt against someone and somebody is hated, libelled, mentioned with evil-aimed, at least negative adjectives. And sometimes scorned too. Criticism is created, fabricated, even invented. This is a need.

The reason for this need can be jelaousy, an inferiority complex, a psychological or mental tension. So, let's assume that those who do not like Jews are the majority in the world. Are followers of other religions any better loved? What do French feel towards Germans? Let's open up the world map. Half of the countries have inimicous sentiments towards the other half. In the civilized Europe, there are senseless ones who shout out that Turks shall not be accepted into the European Union just because they are Muslims. What are we going to call them? Antiislamists? Or was Europe turned in the last fifty years into "the single toothed monster, called civilization"?

Is it only countries who are opposite to the opposite? Parties inside countries, groups inside parties, persons inside groups. Hostility in families. What is clearly visible is this; people search for a reason to be against each other and they find it as well. Let's not forget those with a hidden agenda in the establishment of hostile feelings. The United Nations was founded in 1945. Ever since, sixty-five wars erupted and the great UN could not prevent any of these. Or rather, overlooked them and maybe even winked at them.

Whatever is to be done, it is not possible to soothe "anti" sentiments. An example... You jump in the air and hold a flying bird with your mouth. The "anti" will complain: You should have held two. Antiislamism, antichristianism, antisemitism and others, we will get used to living together. Otherwise, what a pity!

I DON'T KNOW MUCH ABOUT MUSIC

However, I love music. And there are probably no one who does not love music, it is not possible. Each breathing creature that we call an animal likes a sort of music. They have to, because this is the way they are created. It is known that plants like music as well. They say, if you sing while watering them, plants lean lightly forward and salute you and that they even smile.

What is music? It is a branch of art a person makes to express his feelings with sounds. Sound means in Physics a vibration. Sentimentally, we say music is food for the soul. We had learned it at school. If we say, "Music is born from the agreement between melody, rythm and harmony", would we not reflect the truth?

Music means sound, so what is silence? Silence is the opposite of sound; where there is sound, silence can establish itself too. An example: The American composer John Cage has a piano work called 4.33. Dear musician and pianist Fazıl Say explains te work as such: "The pianist enters the stage. He salutes the audience and sits, lifts the piano's cover, waits. Then he closes the cover, waitns, then he opens it up again. He waits again. Then he closes it, then opens it. He does it a few times, when the 4 minutes and 33 seconds are over, he closes the cover, gets up, salutes the audience and returns to the backstage."

This work stems from the "Listening to the silence" in the Indian philosophy. Everyone in the audience, including the pianist, lends an ear to the sound that does not exist. When the cover of the piano opens, the first part starts, when it closes, it sneds. In the second opening of the cover, the second part starts. This opening and closing lasts until 4 minutes 33 seconds are over. Meanwhile, all the sounds in the hall are included into the piece. May be a sneeze... People mumbling nicely, what is this pianist doing, what does he think he is doing...

This melody of silence was offered to us on our 25th marriage anniversary. It was so meaningful... The guests were first surprised. Then they applauded. Silence is as valuable as the sound. Silence is golden they say, and this can be counted as a proof. Isn't that a sense of respect to the audience toabstinate from spoiling silence with bad sounds?

Let's close our eyes, close our ears to the sounds coming from the outside and let's turn inside. Maybe we live a very beautiful experience. Music does not ask us to understand it, it suffices that we like it. Music explains the human being, it tells about the humanity. Whatever style it is, not loving music is like not being alive.

AN ERROR CORRECTED

When I saw it for the first time I felt there was something wrong in that text. Words were placed on a wall without even paying attention to their meaning. In our country, this is to be considered ordinary. It is true that we are not being very careful while using our language, while talking or writing. Just like the famous story says, "I made it."And we seek consolation in it. I never forget what my -now deceased- boss said: "Making a mistake is human, repeating the mistake is devilish" he said. Making a mistake is unescapable, but it was necessary to correct that text on the wall. But how?

First I should have been sure. Was there really a mistake on that text? Or was it just my opinion? Woh was I learn this? By asking someone whose knowledge and teaching about Turkish I trust...

So I sent the e-mail below to Feyza Hepçilingirler, one of Cumhuriyet's columnists on September 04, 2008:

In the middle of Beşiktaş, at the seaside, on a wall seeing the main alley, this text is written wirh quite big letters: TBMM National Palaces Warehouse – Museum

Thousands of cars and pedestrians pass by this text every day. Isn't that more correct to say "Archive-Museum" instead of "Warehouse-Museum"? I guess things are archived in the National Palaces. Isn't the word "Warehouse" more suitable to residences, or to the industry and trade?

I send a photo of the text attached. I would love to learn your opinion on this subject. Thank you very much for your interest.

Reading the Cumhuriyet Newspaper is my father's legacy on me. I have this pleasure since more than half a century. I was curious. What was Feyza Hoca going to say when she received this e-mail? Maybe she would write to the related offices or have someone at the newspaper tell about it? Maybe – but a very small chance- she would find it unworthy to mention. When I was returning from my holidays in Izmir two months ago, I have seen that the text on the wall was now shortened. The words "Warehouse-Museum" were taken off, which had in my opinion corrected the mistake.

Dear Ms. Hepçilingirler also replied my e-mail. I have read it on her column on December 18, 2008. Here I present it:

Yakup Almelek also sent me a photo of the inscription on the wall of a building seeing the main alley, at the sea side in Beşiktaş: TBMM NATIONAL PALACES WARE-HOUSE – MUSEUM

I write here the meaning of the word "warehouse": "- A place where something is placed in order to protect it, store it and use it when necessary. 2- A place where a good is sold wholesale. 3- A place where army goods are stored and maintained (TDK Turkish Discitonary). As Yakup Almelek is saying, everything in the National Palaces must have been archived. Than, isn't it more appropriate to call is an "archive" instead of a "warehouse"?

I would like to thank Dear Feyza Hepçilingirler for her interest.

Dear Readers,

Either a warehouse or an archive, does it make a difference? Not at all. Life goes on, but our language is a beautiful language and what would we have if we cared a bit more while speaking and writing? We would have an even more beautiful language.

I wish that all our readers enjoy the new year the way they please.

AN ABSOLUTE MUST TO SAY

Bensiyon Pinto's language; Tülay Gürler's pen
One told and the other wrote
And this shining work came up.
The story of a life
I congratulate both of them, w tih all my heart.
We have a common side with Bensiyon.
We were born in the same year
But I am six months older than him.
Don't ever mention age to Bensiyon
He may be sore, angry and even cut ropes with you.
A book came to life, its name fits its objective.
His memoire will remain on the bookshelves of every
Turkish Jew
And what our honorary president has done, must be
exemplary
Why did other presidents hide their life so far
Why did they not share their experience
We would learn our society more, the more we read.
A road opened up in front, now they will walk
Now the presidents will follow each other
They will offer what they now, and to the youth in
particular.
It is hard to be a Jew.
To stand against a thousand hardships
End everything has a price in life
It is expensive

To remain in a minority
One by one, each were considered
In between lines.
We have to love the land we live in
We have to be brave
We have to be patient
All of these are
İn the dictionary of humankind
The Wealth Tax was bitter, The 6-7 September sorrowful
No Turk bearing a heart in his chest
Approved them
Six million jews were murdered
In the second war, in front of all eyes,
In front of an audience
Where were the other Westerners
Were they having a nap?
Closeness, interest, loyalty is there
What is sacrifice! There is fairness and comprehension
In "An Absolute Must to Say"...

ATATÜRK AND THE LITTLE CHILD

November 10, 1938 Ankara,

Yeğenbey District, in other words the Jewish Quarter.

"Atatürk is dead", "Atatürk is dead."

Her mother had leaned in front of a tub, washing laundry. Upon hearing these words, her body calcified. She got up with difficulty. She took her head between her hands. She looked down, where the voice was coming from. In the sofa stood his aunt. She was the one telling these words. His mother asked with a trembling voice "Is he dead?" The aunt shook her head, meaning yes... She started to cry. His mother could no longer contain herself. Her tears poured down her cheeks. In a few minutes, his grandmothers were coming from the main door. They were also in tears.

One was asking herself and around "What are we to do now?" No one around was in the condition to give an answer. A few women from the neighbours came into the courtyard. Their faces were wet. The child was three years old. To those who asked his age, he would show his three fingers and sat three, three. Because his father had taught him to do so.

He saw a dream that night. It was an unforgettable experience. While sleeping tight, the painting in the living room came to life. This was the painting, his sister mentioned as Atatürk's picture. The handsome soldier in the painting smiles at him, and he responds by smiling back. He felt his face blush from embarassment. He will remember the conversation between Atatürk and him all his life...

Atatürk asked, "Are you okay?" Encouraged by Atatürk's smile, he replied "I am upset with you" Atatürk's eyebrows slightly contract. "Why," he asked, "what have I done to you?"

The child replies on the spot, "Because you died. Because you died my mother, my grandmothers and the entire street cried. If you had not died, they would not have cried."Atatürk replied, "Yes, you are right. I should not have died." "Please, do not die anymore" said the child. "Promise me not to die anymore." "Allright," said Atatürk, "If you don't want me to die, I won't die."

The child suddenly asks: "Do you have any children?"

"Yes," says Atatürk.

"How many?"

"Millions" replies Atatürk.

"How much is millions"

"How far can you count?" asks Atatürk.

The child replies proudly "I know how to count until five. See, one, two, three, four, five."

"Bravo," says Atatürk. "You counted right."

The child insists; "How much is millions?"

Atatürk replies, "It is many, many times five."

The child narrowed his eyes. It was apparent that he wanted to reach the millions, but when he realized that this is not easy, he wanted to change the topic;

"Will you play with me?" he asked.

And he rejoices upon Atatürk's answer "Yes, I will." Excited, "Listen, Atatürk" he said, "Now I should sleep, then I should get up and brush my teeth. Otherwise my mom will shout at me, then I will eat my meal. Then if I call you, would you come?"

"I would."

The child looks at Atatürk in admiration: "I am my mother's child, I am my father's child, can I be your child too?"

Atatürk: "Yes, I would love that."

Upon this answer, the child opened his arms wide and shouted "Atatürk, I love you so much!"

Atatürk opened his arms and said "My child, I love you too." The child approached Atatürk with his arms wide open and they hugged. Suddenly, the child saw himself in the mirror as a youth, suddenly he saw himself with gray hair, suddenly, he saw himself with white hair.

Atatürk was always by his side and looked at him with a shining smile in his eyes.

IT IS NECESSARY TO SMILE ONCE IN A WHILE

A few days ago, I met a Şalom reader on the way. We chatted a bit. He pointed at an issue: "You mentioned humour in your article called "Laughter on the Job" but you didn't give any examples" he said.

And he was absolutely right.

Never a truer word spoken. Laughter on the Job is a four paged bulletin and it is published by Alper Almelek every three months. Anecdotes about business life, jokes, caricatures and some humourous maxims. In these words, there is no race, no religion, no sex, no obscenity and no strong words. (They were collected in a book by Alfa Yayınları).

Let's move away from the bulletin for a change. Do you think the belowmentioned is humour?

Let's say you invited a friend to an afternoon tea. While your guest is eating the fruit cake you have offered, your wife praises the *kapusta* she has cooked in the morning. And so that your guest doesn't miss this wonderful taste, you bring a plate full of *kapusta*.

What shall he do! Would you eat a fruit cake and a cabbage dish together? But it is a duty of the guest. Shall he eat it or not? Is this act carrying elements of humour? In a theater play, such a scene can carry humouristic elements and the guest's reaction can make the audience laugh. Its interpretation is up to you...

Now let's return to Laughter on the Job.

The human brain is an awesome organ. In the morning, it starts working the moment one wakes up and it doesn't stop until you come to work. What does it mean? It means, in a funny way, our brain stops the moment we enter our office. If so, it is wiser to take decisions about business outside of business... Maybe when we wake up in our bed, or while taking a stroll. In an environment where our brain is sparkly... Let's leave this topic to its specialists and move to another branch. Here's an interesting excerpt from Laughter on the Job.

If two persons are always of the same opinion about business, then one of them is useless. If they are always of opposite opinions about a business, then both of them are useless. This could be a hypothesis which could be applied to any political party in the world. Its proposal is that political parties may need to have the same orientation when it comes to certain issues. The same is also ideal in commercial partnerships.

Now a tragic end... There is no doubt advertisement brings quick results. Yesterday we had posted a job ad for a security personnel. In the same night we were robbed. What do you say to this? A good secretary should do much more than dictating, using a keyboard and making coffee. She should at the same time create the image that her boss is always on the job.

MY GOD, WHERE ARE YOU?

Year 1951, maybe 1952. In the summer months when the schools in Ankara were on holiday, I was working at a stationery called "Tan". Then, that place was called "Taşhan". Then it became "Ulus". When could a 14-15 years-old boy do in a small business? Let me explain. Mopping the floor, cleaning the windows and when it's all over, being a cashier.

I had yet another job: delivery. Placing the stationery orders placed usually by embassies into a taxi, taking them to their address and delivering them... This was painstaking. Especially in July, the sun is scorching in our capital city.

Our personnel consisted of three people, me included. The big boss lived in Istanbul. He was barely coming to Ankara once a month. The small boss was Moiz Abi. He was the company responsible. I liked him, for he was a nice person. He would treat me like an adult. He would talk to me, ask questions and tell me things. I would consider myself as an important person. Once he even gave me a secret. He told me he loved the daughter of someone known in the Jewish Community of Ankara and that he intended to marry her; he asked me to keep it as a secret. Later on he married that girl.

With the incident that I will tell not, we will get a hint about the title of my article.

One day, I have brought the stationary order of an embassy in various packages by stopping a taxi on the street. There were four packs of A4 paper in the order. The Taxi had left the packaged at the security line and I had to carry them one by one into the building. Then I saw that the papers were left in the car. This was impossible for the ignoble taxi driver not to see the packaged as they were on the side seat.

The embassy official told the issue to Moiz Abi on the phone. I was very sorry. I remember having made an effort so that no one saw me crying while returning to the shop by bus. Back then paper was not being produced in the country. Everything was imported and everything was very expensive. "Deduct it from my weekly pay" I had said to my bosses but they replied "no". "Since it was the first time, we forgive you."

I told the incident to my parents. "Raise up all your antennas the next time" said my father. It was heavy. Suddenly I figured. I was going to find that taxi. My eyes were now on the street while going to work and on the weekends. I was praying every day to God, "Please, help me find that car!" My father was having fun with me. The second World War was over five, six years ago. Millions had died. A part of those who lost their lives were children. During the war my father would follow the French radio and exclaim, "My God, where are you!" We had heard him and we had feared. My father told me, "God did not move a finger against that savagery. Now will he help you find your five packs of paper?"

What he had heard had turned him into a non-believer. And until he died, he did not perform any of his religious duties. But I think it was one month past, and I have seen the taxi one day, when we were in Çankaya together with a few friends strolling down. After a dispute, I noted his number plate and Moiz Abi complained to the Police Directorate of Ulus. The driver had paid the cost.

This simple incident has left an impression on me. My father's interpretation of the event was, "This is just a coincidence, it has nothing to do with God."

Was it really the case? My father must have found out when he reached the hereafter. I am curious. When it is my turn, I will also learn the secret.

AFİFE JALE

The word Afife means honest, clean, respectable. It is known that Afife Jale is worthy of all these titles. However Afife had a disadvantage. She was a woman. Until the proclamation of the Republic, it was a crime for a woman to appear on the stage. What wqas expected from a woman at that time! Marry, bear children, cook delicious meals for your husband, keep yourself busy with ironing and laundry. Don't even try to do a man's job. Even today, that's what most of the men think.

Afife Jale was the granddaughted of Dr. Sait Paşa. She was born in 1902 in Istanbul. She was the first Turkish girl accepted to the Darulbedayi by examination, on November 10th, 1938. She was, among other ladies, the only one who was appointed as a junior artist for a monthly salary of 500 Kurush. Howver, she was looked down at by men, not considered for a role and even harassed.

The play "Odalık" (Concubine) she appeared on at the Apollon Theater of Kadıköy in 1920 was raided by the police because "a Muslim girl was on the stage!" Afife was smuggled through the boiler room and taken to the theater owner's house. Next year, in 1921, it was prohibited for Muslim women to appear on stage. Despite this and by opposing bravely to the reactions of some, she worked with private troops such as Yeni Tiyatro, Milli Sahne and Türk Tiyatrosu.

In these years, she married Selahattin Pınar, who produced unforgettable works of Turkish music. Pınar has composed the song "Nereden Sevdim O Zalimi" (How did I love that crual woman) for Jale, with whom he was madly in love. Afife Jale was tired. She was in a continuous psychological battle. She started to use drugs. They took him to Bakırköy Psychiatric Hospital. And on July 23, 1941, she left this world. Is it possible to forget Afife Jale? No. Yapı Kredi Sigorta is emphasizing its love and respect to the first Muslim actress of Turkey, with the Afife Jale Prizes it has started to distribute.

Among those who keep Afife Jale living in their hearts and souls is also Haldun Dormen, who is an important personality. Besides, a movie about her is also on the news. Produced by Makara film, the movie is directed by Ceyda Aslı Kılıçkıran. Renowned artists are playing in this movie. For example, Müjde Ar, Ayla Algan, M.Ali Alabora and others we may want to watch with pleasure... Is it a sentimental coincidence? Maybe it is. Müjde Ar had interpreted Afife Jale in 1987. 20 years later, the role belongs to her again. Together with Çiğdem Suyolcu.

The name of the movie is "Kilit". The scenario belongs to Kılıçkıran as well, it has a very interesting subject, which, while judging yesterday, evokes today and related to reencarnation. Two women, Afife and Berna. The pain, humiliation and fear women of their personality suffer were depicted. Nowadays actresses are being applauded everywhere in Turkey. Maybe Afife Jale sees it, with eyes full of tears.

I would like to thank Ceyda Aslı Kılıçkıran for the clarifications she has sent over e-mail.

CARL EBERT

Contrary to the widespread belief, Carl Ebert was not Jewish. No doubt about that, one does not need to be a Jew in order to oppose to the Nazi cruelty or to Hitler. It is enough to be a human.

Carl Ebert was a human. Not with the bare meaning in the dictionaries, not in the appearance, but he was essentially a human. A real German, a real personality, a real European and a real world citizen. This was the way he was to be defined. This was what his spiritual identity gave out.

He was born in 1887 in Berlin. He studied theater. He became the general art director of the Berlin Opera in 1931. In 1933, when he started to criticize the Hitler government, he was laid off. He fled to Argentina. He was invited to Turkey by Atatürk in 1936. He remained in Ankara for 10 years. What has he done in Ankara?

He developed the State Theater and the Conservatory in Ankara. He made them contemporary and he trained students. From among these students, valuable professors teached later on. On the 120th year of his birth, in a panel organized in Istanbul Profilo Center, his students told about Carl Ebert with love and respect. And the audience accompanied them with applauses. Refik Erduran, who gained the viewer's and the reader's acclaim with his plays and column articles, was directing the panel. He was not a student of Ebert, but a very valuable theater artist, Can Gürzap talked about him too. Ayten Gökçer read the letter Cüneyt Gökçer had written for his professor Carl Ebert. He was defining the great Ebert in such a magnificent way. Sincere and pure.

With her self-criticism and sympathetic allure, Macide Tanır was by one word a chef d'oeuvre that day. I am sorry if the word chef d'oeuvre is insufficient, as I could not find another way to describe her. The Dean of the Culture University of Istanbul was mentioned his appreciation of Ebert too. When I saw Prof. Mesut İktu among the panellists, I had first thought that we were going to enjoy a musical feats but the professor preferred to talk. Later on, we found on that the musical feast was to be given bt Suat Arıkan and his accompanyist. We heard arias, which we loved one more than the other one. Our ears rejoiced this feast.

Those who like theater and opera should be thankful to Emre Erdem who organized the evening. I was a witness of how much he worked and how the "No"s did not discourage him and how hard he tried in order to find those who say "Yes". And he made it.

Erdem held a short speech. In this speeach, it was nice and elegant of him to present his thankfulness to the sponsors. It was beautiful that he thanked Tilda Levi, a prominent voice from the Şalom Newspaper. As a Şalom columnist, I should say I felt proud. Viki Habif was among names he did not forget to mention.

The Ankara State Theater and Conservatory should protect Carl Ebert's legacy. A memorial day in the year would be considered examplary by the generations of today and tomorrow. Those who know Carl Ebert express his human side. Let's commemorate him with a poetry called Song of Mankind

Humanity is an ideal, hardest to reach
A crescent in the endlessness, on the beloved horizon
We are masons, a mitre and a compass in our hands
We run behind the light, our name is beauty
Without knowing religion or race, we are equal brothers
Let's sing songs, humanity is our objective
Humanity is our resolution.

BEING CONTEMPORARY

Modernization is one of the most difficult targets to attain. A mental and psychic condition necessitating to go forward every day, or to be at least aware of it. It is possible to define it this way, but until where or when? Until where and when the life ends. Being modern means knowing today, what today is and knowing tomorrow what tomorrow is.

The same goes for the national economy, politics and business life. And in the arts, not much is different in that ocean neither. In order to continue to exist, the individual should be up-to-date. No alternative is possible. All problems stem from a lack of being contemporary

If we are not contemporary, we remain in the yesterday. And than yesterday becomes day before. Gradually, we get extinct and we disappear. Being contemporary is in a way being modern. Here we can meet a dilemma, since so many persons and institutions claim to be modern. Who can rightly embrace modernity? Not with words or concepts, but with signs, in other words, only a person acting contemporary by obeying the rules of a thinking mind, should embrace this right. If we clarify, isn't an attitude modern or contemporary, only when it shows pure reality, without beinding towards demagogy and polemic? It is, but on the condition of being open to novelties.

In politics, this is a difficult business... Demagogy means agitating, firebranding. A salad of words is as useful as it gets in the content of making politics. Expecting a politician to catch the time! It is also difficult in economics because part of the economics is feeding with politics. In some countries, it even became an inseparable part of the other one. When one looks at the economy, one also sees politics.

Since being contemporary is the product of an individual effort, it can be best realized in art. For example in visual arts, in painting, sculpture or in ceramics, the artist may learn by seeing and see and do by practicing and reach a modern level. It is the same in architecture. Here the process is very important! It is necessary to grasp which phases were experienced in that art, even at a glance, starting from the early ages. For example, is it possible to grasp the modern without knowing the classic? Theater is yet another ocean. The university of civilization. An art, depicting the yesterday and today of society and individuals. Its aim is to remain contemporary forever. The theater writer believes to fulfil his duty this way.

SECRET

At the entrance of the Epcot Center building in Orlando, which is a technological wonder containing the fine art called Disney World as well, a sentence welcomes the viewers.

This sentence consisting of nine words is a real pathfinder. It is actually a lighthouse shedding light to the worries of many young people... what is this magic? Please read! "If you can dream it, you can do it!"

This sentence was a best friend openind the gate of success to many. Many people who could reach it do not hide it. Some of them even write about it. Here I will digress to mention a book that I have read. It s called "Secret". I think this book has got its verve from the nine words above.

What is this? Let's oncover the secret on the title of the book.

The big secret of our dream is contained in the law of attraction. You attract things that spring to your mind or things you think about. Ideas are magnetic and they have frequences. We send these to the universe and attract those with the same frequence. If we send good thoughts, the returning ones will be of the same frequence. So, if we would like to change something in our life we should also change our thoughts about that thing. The law of attraction is basically "similar things attract each other." If we think about bad things, bad ideas go to the cosmos and bad ideas return to us. Can we human beings see ourselves as radio antennas sending and receiving frequences? Yes. This is what the Secret claims.

Dear Readers, I remember an article I had read a longtime ago. The human brain distributes electromagnetic waves. Of course, these waves have lengths. Good orators can keep the audience with the length of their waves under their influence.

Let's keep on uncovering this "secret" which is kept hidden...

What are we thinking?

It depends on how we feel.

So, can we change our feelings?

Yes, we can.

How?

By changing certain factors.

How is that going to be?

By listening to a piece of music that we love, by reading an article that interests us, by smelling the perfume of nature, for example, by viewing the wonderful scenery of the Bosphorus we can change our feelings. Our feelings change our thoughts and most importantly, they create happiness.

Yes. It all depends on the law of attraction.

Aren't these hints about the secret? This is the only hypothesis in the book. I am sure the writer of the book will oppose about the word "hypothesis".

Dear Readers,

It is possible to tell about the book with 400-450 words, but then, the article would be so concentrated and introverted, I would fear that you take your eyes away. The author of the book is an American mother of two. Her name is Rhonda Byrne. The book has many sides open to criticism as well but one thing is that the book has a quality worth discussing about.

I do not know whether dedicating the next few articles to this topic would be a sensible idea.

We are entering winter, let it be reasonably cold!

DO YOU LIKE CATS?

Dear Readers,

Do you like cats? Would you take a cat in your arms and cuddle him? Whould let him smear his paws to your face? Would you rub his belly? I should honestly sat i, I don't like cats. Or, rather: I didn't like cats. Until I have read Doris Lessing's book "On Cats". When I say I didnt like them, of course this should not mean that I ever maltreated them.

So, who is Doris Lessing? What is this for a book, such that after reading it, people start feeling a sympathy and even love towards cats? Dosir Lessing is an Englishwoman aged 88. She was born in Iran and migrated to Africa when she was 5 with her family. She remained in a farm in Rhodesia until she was 30. After working at several trades, she decided to become a writer. Apparently a good choice, since whe was awarded with the Nobel Prize on Literature this year.

Be it for humans or for animals, one should not make a judgement about them without knowing them well. For cats, they say they are "ungrateful animals". They say cats forget about the value of a favor done for them. But how much do we know cats? Those that Lessing tells do not take me to such an impression. Quite the opposite, cats are apparently proud and loving personalities.

Another thing. Cats apparently attach a lot of importance to humans. They want to be liked by humans. While their meowing sometimes means a complaint, it could also be an effort to draw fellow humans' attention to them. Just like so many bipedal creatures striving to be loved.

May God give her a long life, Lessing is with cats since she was five, so since 83 years. She always had cat(s) at home.

She was both their owner and their friend. Sometimes she loved them and sometimes she was angry at them. While she was learning a lot of things from them she teached them a lot of things. Lessing does not only tell about cats in general, she also tells how they lived together under one roof. So her observations are based on truth and experience.

Did we know that cats decide to die? Yes, when they are ill and when they lose their power to struggle, they crawl to a calm place and wait in dignity that their last hour comes. Proudly, without complaining.

And who told that cats are ungrateful? They give a cat who was used to her home and to her owner to a lumberjack. The lumberjack takes the cat to a mountain house located 30 kms apart. The cat meows, she is not happy but no one cares. The next day the lumberjack phones and tells that the cat is lost. The cat returns fifteen days later to her beloved home and mistress. She is hungry, thirsty, angry, weakened, her fur scruffy, her eyes crazy and full of fear. How could she make that thirty kilometers in two weeks? There was no straight road, how could she cross random pahtways and thick shrubs? Moreover she had crossed two rivers. Wasn't that a miracle that she could find her home? Did she swim across the rivers? Her instincts had guided her. There could be no other reason. And when the cat was back home she looked at her owner a long time. It was as if she was saying: "How could you give me to a stranger?" Then she jumped into her arms, she purred and she cried in happiness.

Do you like cats? I don't like cats but I like dogs. I have heard this sentence many times. I used to say the same thing too. But apparently we were wrong... We should say sorry to our cats.

I HAVE TO BE THE NUMBER ONE!

Son: Dad, I want to talk to you.

Father: That would be good, you with your school and I with my business, we cannot come together very often.

Son: This year I will take the university entrance exams but I don't think I will be successful. And I am not prepared. When I see my friends, they all look in better condition than I. They received private lessons or visited courses. I ididn't do anything.

Father: And what are you coming up with this?

Son: You are resembling university entrance exams to a horse race. I am not a horse.

Father: No, you are not. But It doesn't seem probable that conditions are changing anytime soon. Do you have an alternative, how do you plan to study?

Son: I want to study in the US.

Father: Why US?

Son: I want to study music. In Istanbul, they do not admit me to the conservatory because of my age. We were a few friends who have already asked this.

Father: You are ambitious about it, both your mother and I can see this. What do you want to become with music, a pianist?

Son: I want to take composition and song courses together with piano. Give my this chance, you will see that I will be very successful.

Father: Allright, but I have three conditions.

Son: I will accept the conditions whatever they are.

Father: First; if you want to earn your bread with art you have to be one of the best, and even the best. For example, you should reach the level of Fazıl Say. I think being a concert pianist is a very difficult job. It requires and awful load of work and sacrifice... You should never forget this. The objective is to become no "1".

Son: You will see I will do it. What is the second condition?

Father: You will not fail the class. If the conservatory is four years, you should complete it in four years. If you fail, you return that very year!

Son: Why should I. I have always passed my class with honors.

Father: I just do my duty of reminding. The third condition is, we hear bad things about America. Like using drugs, or being dragged into an inappropriate relationship.

Son: Dad, how could you think of such things about me? I always knew what I was doing. Don't worry, really...

Father: There is no harm in talking about things in advance.

Son: Allright dad, can I ask you something?

Father: Go ahead.

Son: Should one be the best only in art? Isn't that the same thing in other professions?

Father: No, it isn't. For example, in business life, even if you are not the best as an employee or a business owner, you can still have a good life. You can earn the living of your family. You don't need to become a Sakıp Sabancı, Vehbi Koç or Nejat Eczacıbaşı. Is it the same in art? Unfortunately not.

If one does not become one of the best in music, just like in visual arts or in literature, then one has to search for an additional resource of finance. These are treacherous occupations asking for perseverance and ambition. They always look for the very best.

Son: You are right, dad.

•••

Dear Readers. How shall we end this litle story? Shall the young man go to American and return as a successful pianist? Or shall he realize, after remaining there for a couple of years, that he is not going to become one of the best and change profession? We can also advice the young man in our story this: Just have a profession and keep art among your best loved hobbies.

Please place the full stop yourselves.